The AMERICAN GIRLS PARTY BOOK

YOU'RE INVITED!

PLEASANT COMPANY PUBLICATIONS

Published by Pleasant Company Publications
© Copyright 1998 by Pleasant Company
All rights reserved. No part of this book may be used or reproduced in
any manner whatsoever without written permission except in the case of
brief quotations embodied in critical articles and reviews. For information,
address: Book Editor, Pleasant Company Publications,
8400 Fairway Place, P.O. Box 620998, Middleton, WI 53562.

Printed in the United States of America.
99 00 01 02 03 04 WCR 10 9 8 7 6 5 4

PICTURE CREDITS
The following individuals and organizations have generously given
permission to reprint images in this book:
1—Jeffry Myers/FPG International LLC; 8—Talbot County (Maryland) Historical Society; 10—Colonial
Williamsburg Foundation; 15—Sterling Silver and Crystal courtesy of Janet's Antiques, Madison, WI (top);
JAL659 *Adoration of the Kings* by Diego Rodriguez de Silva y Velázquez (1599-1660), Prado, Madrid/Bridgeman
Art Library, London/New York (bottom); 17—PWI89752 *Girl with Racket and Shuttlecock* by Jean-Baptiste
Simeon Chardin (1699-1779), Louvre, Paris, France/Bridgeman Art Library, London/New York, Credit Peter
Willi; 27—Condé Nast Publications;
29—Nacimiento courtesy of Carol Ann and Max Howell; 33—Henry Ford Museum & Greenfield Village,
Neg. #72.192.30 (bottom left); 1943.8.12636 and 1943.8.12641. (CONN-CA-28)/IA: Calvin, Robert. Index of
American Design, ©1998 Board of Trustees, National Gallery of Art, Washington (bottom right); 41—Abby
Aldrich Rockefeller Folk Art Center, Williamsburg, VA; 43—Pitcher courtesy of *bennington potters;
44—Quintet Publishing Limited (bottom left); Department of Special Collections, General Library System,
University of Wisconsin–Madison (bottom right); 47—Courtesy of Alex G. Malloy, Inc.; 51—Illustration by
Marty Norman from Peter L. Skolnik's *Jump Rope!* Copyright © 1974 by Peter L. Skolnik. Workman Publishing
Co., Inc., New York. All rights reserved; 52—Mug courtesy of *bennington potters; 54-55—Pitcher and cups
courtesy of Joan Diehl; 58—State Historical Society of Wisconsin (bottom); 60—Images reproduced from *The
Complete Book of Pressed Flowers* with permission from Penny Black and DK Publishing, Inc.; 61—Hartford
Steam Boiler Inspection & Insurance Company; 64—Goblets courtesy of Joan Diehl; 65—Robert Opie
Collection (bottom); 70—Corbis-Bettmann; 71—Corbis-Bettmann (bottom left); illustration by Nick Backes
(bottom right); 77—DeSoto Brown Collection (top right and middle left); 80—Papyrotamia patterns from
Colonial America by Susan Schneck and Mary Strohl. Published by Scholastic Professional Books. ©1991 by
Scholastic Inc. Used by permission.

Written by Michelle Jones
Edited by Jodi Evert and Michelle Jones
Designed and Art Directed by Tricia B. Doherty, Laura Moberly, and Jane S. Varda
Produced by Tracy L. Erickson and Virginia A. Gunderson
Cover Illustrations by Dan Andreasen, Nick Backes, Renée Graef, Dahl Taylor, and Jean-Paul Tibbles
Spot Illustrations by D.J. Simison
Step-by-Step Illustrations by Liz Wheaton
Photography by Connie Russell, Mark Salisbury, Paul Tryba, and Jamie Young
Historical and Picture Research by Rebecca Sample Bernstein,
Kathy Borkowski, Michelle Jones, Debra Shapiro, and Sally Wood
Food and Prop Styling by Jean doPico and Sarajane Lien
Model Styling by Jean doPico
Crafts Made by Chris David, Tricia B. Doherty, Jean doPico,
Virginia A. Gunderson, Sarajane Lien, and June Pratt
Prop Research by Jean doPico

Library of Congress Cataloging-in-Publication Data

The American Girls party book/[edited by Jodi Evert and Michelle Jones; written by Michelle Jones;
inside illustrations by D.J. Simison; photography by Jamie Young . . . et al.]. — 1st ed.
p. cm. — (The American Girls collection)
Summary: Includes ideas and instructions for party decorations, foods, favors, and
games reflecting the worlds of each of the six American Girls: Felicity, Josefina,
Kirsten, Addy, Samantha, and Molly.
ISBN 1-56247-677-7 (pbk.)
1. Children's parties—Juvenile literature. 2. Cookery, American—Juvenile literature.
3. Party decorations—Juvenile literature. 4. Handicraft—Juvenile literature.
[1. Parties. 2. Cookery. 3. Party decorations. 4. Handicraft.]
I. Jones, Michelle. II. Simison, D.J., ill. III. Young, Jamie, ill. IV. Series.
TX731.J68 1998 793.2′1—dc21 98-15582 CIP AC

Table of Contents

Plan a Party   1

Mix and Match   2

Tips for You   4

Felicity
    Colonial Party 6
    New Year's Ball 14
    Plantation Picnic 16

Josefina
    New Mexican Party 18
    Harvest Celebration 26
    Fandango 28

Kirsten
    Prairie Party 30
    Barn Dance 38
    Patchwork Party 40

Addy
    Freedom Party 42
    Summer Fair 50
    Stitch-in-Time Party 52

Samantha
    Victorian Party 54
    Nutting Party .62
    Painting Party .64

Molly
    Home-Front Party 66
    Summer Camp-Out 74
    Hawaiian Hula Party 76

Patterns   78

Special thanks to all the children and parents who tested
the projects and gave us their valuable comments:

Jamie Ausman
Sara Bandt
Caitlin Besadny
Bailey Bintz
Shanna Bodilly
Elizabeth Booth
Monica Bowar
Molly Brosuis
Allison Brummel
Amy Bucci
Laura Bucci
Madeleine Calhoon
Alanna Clarke
Hanna Dehnert
Monika Dehnert
Genieve Dodsworth
Lauryn Durtschi
Catherine Enderlin
Devri Fisher
Susan Frederickson
Amanda Gerland
Anna Goolsby
Lisa Gruenisen
Krista Hagman
Alyssa Hamilton
Lauren Hannifan
Kathryn Hartmann
Kayla Hillerns
Robin Holmquist
Claire Ivanowski
Greta Jordan
Kari Jordan

Colleen Karrigan
Lauren Kirk
Gina Koberle
Katherine Kozarek
Katelyn Lawry
Lauren Merrill
Kacey Mullaney
Ryan Mullaney
Kelsey Nelson
Tiffany Nondahl
Emily Pratt
Heather Preston
Jenna Quarne
Lisa Ragatz
Shelley Roper
Arial Rosenberg
Tori Rosenberg
Danielle Russell
Gabrielle Russell
Katie Schneider
Lily Servais
Maggie Servais
Amanda Smith
Katy Stanton
Vanessa Teff
Kaeli Urben
Lindsay Urben
Emily Werla
April Wheeler
Emily Wolff
Erin Woodward
Laura Woodward
Carrie Zwettler

Lia and Tara Arntsen and their mother Marté Arntsen
Amanda Baldinus and her mother Shirley Baldinus
Erin Bermingham and her mother Patricia Stutz
Kelli Brewster and her mother Debbie Brewster
Katelyn Donisch and her mother Sally Zirbel-Donisch
Kala Jackowski and her mother Susan Jackowski
Chelsea Karns and her mother Karen Karns
Kaela and Kelsey Kluever and their mother Pam Kluever
Molly Lowndes and her mother Mary Anne Lowndes
Beverly Nordin and her mother Barb Nordin
Anne Marie Rego and her mother Sandra Rego
Elise Reinemann and her mother Mary Kay Reinemann
Carlene Schleisman and her mother Joette Schleisman
Tricia Sheahan and her mother Patty Sheahan
Heather Shinstine and her mother Kim Shinstine
Bethany Vander Zouwen and her mother Janice Vander Zouwen
Talia Wipperfurth and her mother Iris Wipperfurth

Plan a Party

Get ready for a great American Girls party!

Since the earliest days of America, American girls have found lots of ways to celebrate—picnics, dances, barn raisings, fairs, teas, and victory shows. In this book, you'll find ideas for planning all these kinds of parties and more. The key to a successful party is to plan ahead. These tips will help you plan a party that's fun for everyone.

Four Weeks Before Your Party:

1. **Choose your party.** Decide what kind of party you would like to have and discuss it with a parent. Decide what the rules will be and where the party will be held.

2. **Choose the date and time.** Talk to a parent about a date and time that works for everyone.

3. **Plan the guest list.** Discuss with a parent how many guests you can invite.

Two Weeks Before Your Party:

4. **Send invitations.** Make the invitations. List anything special you want your guests to bring, such as project supplies, on the invitations. To avoid hurt feelings, never pass out invitations in front of girls who aren't invited to your party.

One Week Before Your Party:

5. **Finalize the guest list.** Call any guests who haven't responded to your invitation.

6. **Make a list.** Write down everything you are planning to do and serve at the party. Then write down exactly what you will need for each of those activities. If you don't have something you need, think of something similar you could use. You just might think of something even better!

The Day Before Your Party:

7. Prepare the food.

8. Decorate the room and set the table.

9. Gather all the materials you will need.

Mix and Match

Host one of the parties shown in this book, or mix and match treats, games, and crafts to create your own American Girls celebration.

	FELICITY	JOSEFINA	KIRSTEN
Treats	Queen Cakes (p. 8) Ginger Cakes (p. 9) Shrewsbury Cakes (p. 9) Candied Flower Petals (p. 9) Liberty Tea (p. 9) Eggnog (p. 15) Twelfth Night Cake (p. 15) New Year's Cookies (p. 15) Lemon Tartlets (p. 16) Chicken Salad (p. 16) Cranberry-Apple Punch (p. 16)	Flan (p. 20) Bizcochitos (p. 21) Lemonade (p. 21) Empanaditas (p. 27) Roasted Pine Nuts (p. 27) New Mexican Hot Chocolate (p. 29) Marquesote (p. 29) Anise Cakes (p. 29)	Prairie Teacakes (p. 32) Lemon Glaze (p. 32) Maple Gingerbread (p. 33) Apple Tarts (p. 33) Ginger Punch (p. 33) Baked Apple Dumplings (p. 39) Corn Bread (p. 39) Apple Cider (p. 39) Patchwork Cake (p. 41) Spiced Chocolate (p. 41) Quilt Square Cookies (p. 41)
Games	Hoop Race (p. 10) The Game of Graces (p. 10) Frog in the Middle (p. 10) Queen Anne and Her Maids (p. 11) Hide the Thimble (p. 11) Hunt the Ring (p. 11) Minuet (p. 14) Quoits (p. 17) Bowls (p. 17) Scotch-Hoppers (p. 17)	The Flower (p. 22) The Rainbow (p. 22) The Coyote and the Fox (p. 23) The Little Burro (p. 23) The Sea Serpent (p. 23) The Little Blind Hen (p. 26) Waltz of the Broom (p. 28)	Puss in the Corner (p. 34) Jackstraws (p. 34) Here I Bake, Here I Brew (p. 34) I Have a Basket (p. 35) Fox and Geese (p. 35) Honey Pot (p. 35) Old Dan Tucker (p. 38) Snap Apple (p. 39) Apple Dance (p. 39) Cat's Cradle (p. 40)
Crafts	Parchment Invitation (p. 7) Stenciled Name Cards (p. 7) Fruit Pyramid Centerpiece (p. 7) Bilboquet (p. 12) Stenciled Place Mats (p. 13) Papyrotamia (p. 13) Fan Invitation (p. 14) Sweet-Smelling Invitation (p. 16)	Ramillete Invitation (p. 19) Framed Name Cards (p. 19) Majolica Pot (p. 24) Cornhusk Flowers (p. 25) Corn Invitation (p. 26) Dancing Slippers Invitation (p. 28)	Bonnet Invitation (p. 31) Hay Bale Name Cards (p. 31) Calico Kitten (p. 36) Straw Horse (p. 37) Barn Invitation (p. 38) Harmonica (p. 38) Patchwork Invitation (p. 40) Handkerchief Doll (p. 40)

ADDY

Benne Candy (p. 44)
Tangy Iced Tea (p. 45)
Fruity Ice Cream (p. 45)
Mini Sweet Potato Pies (p. 45)
Strawberry Shortcake (p. 50)
Fruit Pies (p. 50)
Lemonade (p. 50)
Pincushion Cupcakes (p. 52)
Butterscotch Milk (p. 52)
Sew Sweets (p. 52)

SAMANTHA

Jam Tart Cookies (p. 56)
Victoria Sponge (p. 57)
Ice Cream Bombes (p. 57)
Cucumber Sandwiches (p. 57)
Hot Tea Punch (p. 57)
Nut Sandwiches (p. 63)
Nut-Crunch Apples (p. 63)
Apple Cider (p. 63)
Painted Cookies (p. 64)
Water Color (p. 64)
Artist's Palette Cake (p. 64)

MOLLY

Sugarless Apple Pie (p. 68)
Quick Chocolate Cake (p. 69)
Fruit Fizz (p. 69)
Doughboys (p. 74)
Pigs in a Blanket (p. 74)
S'mores (p. 74)
Hawaiian Banana Bread (p. 76)
Tropical Twists (p. 76)
Fruit Kabobs (p. 76)

Ribbon's End (p. 46)
Hot Boiled Beans (p. 46)
Feather (p. 46)
Little Sally Walker (p. 47)
Shadow Buff (p. 47)
Jump Rope (p. 51)
Beanbag Contest (p. 53)

Whispers (p. 58)
Taboo (p. 58)
Throwing the Smile (p. 58)
Tea Table (p. 59)
Teapot (p. 59)
Read Tea Leaves (p. 59)
Walnut Shell Fortunes (p. 62)
Drawing Game (p. 65)
Tableaux Vivants (p. 65)

Musical Flags (p. 70)
Prisoner's Base (p. 70)
Flag Relay (p. 70)
Red Rover (p. 71)
Statues (p. 71)
Pom-Pom-Pull-Away (p. 71)
Shoot Marbles (p. 73)
Flashlight Tag (p. 75)
Sprint Tug-of-War (p. 75)
Pitch a Tent (p. 75)
Limbo (p. 77)
The Hula (p. 77)

Banner Invitation (p. 43)
Lantern Name Cards (p. 43)
Tissue Paper Flowers (p. 43)
Spool Puppet (p. 48)
Bean Doll (p. 49)
Fair Booth Invitation (p. 50)
Juggling Balls (p. 51)
Spool Card (p. 52)
Beanbags (p. 53)

Victorian Scrap Invitation (p. 55)
Pressed-Flower Name Cards (p. 55)
Butterfly Napkin Rings (p. 55)
Fern Candle (p. 60)
Pressed Flowers and Ferns (p. 60)
Sketchbook (p. 61)
Squirrel Invitation (p. 62)
Nutty Party Favors (p. 62)
Framed Invitation (p. 64)
Paint on Glass (p. 65)

V-Mail Invitation (p. 67)
Star Name Cards (p. 67)
Hanging Flags (p. 67)
Kaleidoscope (p. 72)
Marbles (p. 73)
Tent Invitation (p. 74)
Palm Tree Invitation (p. 76)
Hula Skirt (p. 77)
Lei (p. 77)

Tips for You

Follow these tips for party success.

GENERAL TIPS

*The most important tip for cooking and crafts is to **work with an adult.***

- *Wash your hands with soap before and after your project.*

- *Carefully read the directions all the way through before you start.*

- *Pay attention when using sharp knives and scissors.*

- *Put covers back on containers tightly. If you spill, clean up right away.*

- *Leave your work area as clean as you found it. Wash and dry dishes, put away supplies, and throw away garbage.*

Cooking Tips

1. Gather all the ingredients and equipment you will need before you start to cook. Put everything where you can reach it easily.

2. When you stir or mix, hold the bowl or pan steady on a flat surface, not in your arms.

3. Make sure your mixing bowls, pots, and pans are the right size. If they are too small, you'll probably spill. If pots and pans are too large, foods will burn more easily.

4. Have an adult handle hot pans. Don't use the stove burners or the oven without permission or supervision. Turn off the burner or the oven as soon as a dish is cooked.

5. Potholders and oven mitts will protect you from burns. Use them when you touch anything hot. Protect kitchen counters by putting trivets or cooling racks under hot pots and pans.

6. Keep hot foods hot and cold foods cold. If you plan to make things early and serve them later, store them properly. Foods that could spoil belong in the refrigerator. Wrap foods well.

Craft Tips

1. You can find most of the materials listed in this book in your home or at craft and fabric stores. If an item in the materials list is starred (*), look at the bottom of the list to find out where you can get it. Make sure you have all the supplies you need before the party.

2. If there's a step that doesn't make sense to you, try it out with a piece of scrap paper or fabric first. Sometimes practicing helps.

3. Select a good work area for the craft projects at your party. Pick a place that has plenty of light and is out of reach of pets and younger brothers and sisters.

4. Ask your guests to bring aprons or smocks. When it's time to make crafts, have everyone tie back her hair and roll up her sleeves. Cover the work area with newspapers, and gather all the materials you will need.

5. Get an adult's help when the instructions tell you to. Have an adult help you use tools properly. Don't use the stove or oven without an adult's permission.

6. If the crafts don't turn out exactly like the picture in the book, that's terrific! The pictures are just there to give you ideas. Crafts become more meaningful when you add your own personal touch.

SEWING TIPS

Threading the needle

Wet the tip of the thread in your mouth. Then push the tip through the eye of the needle.

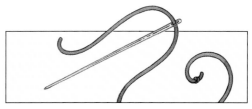

Pull about 5 inches of thread through the needle. Then tie a double knot near the end of the long tail of thread.

Backstitch

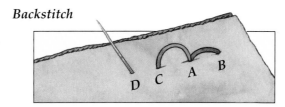

To sew a backstitch, come up at A and go down at B. Come up at C. Then go down at A and come up at D. When you've finished, tie a knot close to your last stitch and cut off the extra thread.

Whipstitch

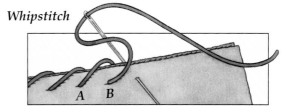

To whipstitch, bring the needle up at A, and then pull the thread over the edge to come up at B. When you've finished, tie a knot close to your last stitch and cut off the extra thread.

Felicity's Color

Share an evening of elegance w...

In Virginia, colonists loved to get together for elegant teas, balls, and other celebrations. They dressed in their fanciest clothes and served their favorite sweets on fine china. Then they played games or danced. Some of their parties lasted for days!

Helena

Miss Jennifer Hanson presents her compliments to Miss Julie Kasper and requests the favor of her attendance at Felicity's Colonial Party at 123 S... meadow Road ... April 15th ...

al Party

ur friends.

Parchment Invitation

Use tan paper that looks like parchment.  Practice the fancy letters and numbers shown on page 78. Write the invitation in your best handwriting, roll it up, and tie it with a ribbon.

Stenciled Name Cards

Fold a 4-by-4 inch piece of paper in half. Tape a small stencil to one corner, leaving room for the name. Use a small sponge to lightly paint the open areas. Let the paint dry, and remove the stencil. Write your guest's name on the card.

Fruit Pyramid Centerpiece

Place a Styrofoam cone (available at craft stores) on a dinner plate. Have an adult cut off the point of the cone. Attach fruit to the cone with toothpicks. Use evergreen boughs or herb sprigs to fill the spaces between the fruit.

7

Tempting Treats

Ask to use your family's best dishes.
Then fill them with colonial goodies.

Dainty queen cakes make delightful party treats.

Queen Cakes

You will need:

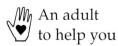 An adult to help you

Ingredients:
Butter to grease pan
Flour to coat greased pan
½ cup butter, softened
½ cup sugar
2 eggs
2 tablespoons rose water*
¼ teaspoon salt
1 cup flour
1 tablespoon flour
¼ cup currants

Equipment:
Paper towels
Muffin pan
Measuring cups
  and spoons
Medium mixing bowl
Wooden spoon
Small bowl
Potholders

*This ingredient is optional. It is available at health-food and import stores and at some supermarkets.

Directions:

1. Preheat the oven to 325°. Use paper towels to grease the muffin pan with butter. Then coat each muffin cup with flour.

2. Cream the butter and sugar together. Beat in the eggs, 1 at a time. Add the rose water and salt. Beat well.

3. Add the cup of flour a little at a time, and beat the mixture well between additions. When all the flour has been added the batter should be smooth.

4. Put 1 tablespoon of flour into the small bowl. Add the currants, and mix until they are coated with flour. Then stir the currants into the batter.

5. Spoon 1 tablespoon of batter into each muffin cup. Divide any remaining batter evenly among the cups.

6. Bake the queen cakes for 40 minutes, or until they are golden brown. Remove from oven and let cool 15 minutes before serving.

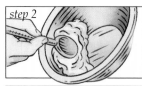
step 2

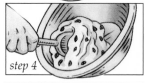
step 4

step 5

Queen cakes were often baked in small heart- or diamond-shaped tins.

8

Ginger Cakes

Ginger cakes are similar to gingersnaps. Make or buy gingersnaps, and use white frosting to frost the cookies.

Liberty Tea

Place 3 teaspoons dried raspberry leaves* in a teapot. Ask an adult to pour 6 cups of boiling water over the leaves. Let the tea steep for 5 minutes. Use a strainer to catch the tea leaves as you pour the tea into teacups. Sweeten the tea with honey and milk.

*Available at health-food and import stores and at some supermarkets.

Shrewsbury Cakes

Shrewsbury cakes are like sugar cookies. Use your favorite sugar cookie dough or a tube of refrigerated cookie dough. Roll out the dough, and use cookie cutters to cut out shapes. If you like, brush the cookies with rose water* before you bake them. The rose water "perfumes" the cakes. Bake the cookies according to the directions.

*Available at health-food and import stores and at some supermarkets.

Candied Flower Petals

Colonists like Felicity decorated their food with flower petals. Buy candied flowers* or make your own. Use violets, roses, and pansies that have never been sprayed with insecticide. Dip the petals in egg whites, and then sprinkle with sugar. Let them dry on a plate overnight. Use decorator icing to add them to your treats.

*Available at baking and import stores.

Games Galore

Your guests will love these colonial party pleasers and teasers!

Hoop Race

Colonial children used the iron hoops from food barrels for toys. Felicity could have gotten a hoop from her father's store. Each racer needs a hoop and a stick. A hula hoop works well. Racers keep their hoops rolling by pushing the hoops along with their sticks.

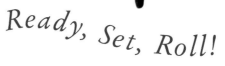

Ready, Set, Roll!

The Game of Graces

Each player has 2 sticks. Dowels from craft or hardware stores work well. The players use the sticks to toss a small hoop, such as an embroidery hoop, back and forth. For fluttery fun, wrap ribbons around the hoop and let the ends hang down as streamers. Keep wrapping ribbons until the entire hoop is covered.

Frog in the Middle

The person who is the Frog sits on a stool. The other players dance around Frog, chanting, "Frog in the middle, you can't catch me!" Frog has to try to catch someone without leaving the stool. The person who's caught becomes the next Frog.

Queen Anne and Her Maids

One person is Queen Anne. She faces the other players and covers her eyes. The Maids stand in a row with their hands behind them. One of them has a ball hidden in her hands. They sing to Queen Anne:

> *"Queen Anne, Queen Anne, she sits in the sun,*
> *As fair as a lily, as brown as a bun;*
> *She sends you three letters,*
> *And begs you'll read one!"*

Queen Anne replies, trying to guess which Maid has the ball:

> *"I cannot read one unless I read all,*
> *So please, Miss _____, deliver the ball!"*

If Queen Anne guesses correctly, the Maid with the ball takes Queen Anne's place. If she guesses wrong, Queen Anne closes her eyes again and another Maid hides the ball.

Hunt the Ring

The players sit on the floor and form a circle around one player. She closes her eyes. The players in the circle keep their hands hidden. They pass a ring back and forth behind their backs. When the player in the center says "stop," she opens her eyes and tries to guess who has the ring. If she guesses right, the players switch places.

Hunt the Ring was a popular forfeit game.

Hide the Thimble

Felicity loved to play this parlor game. All the players leave the room except for one person. She hides a thimble somewhere in the room. Then the group returns to look for it. The person who finds the thimble wins!

FORFEIT GAMES

*Many of the games Felicity played were **forfeit** games. When a player loses a game, she gives up, or forfeits, a small item, like a hair ribbon. When all players have lost at least one item, they choose a player to be the Judge. One by one, the items are held over the Judge's head while the players chant, "Heavy, heavy, what hangs over you?" The Judge announces a penalty, like a somersault. Then the owner of the item performs the penalty to get her item back.*

Colonial Crafts

Crafts like these were great fun for Felicity.

*The English term for the French word **bilboquet** is "bilbo-catcher."*

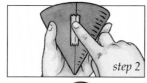

step 1

step 2

step 3

step 4

Bilboquet (BILL-bo-kay)

You will need:

Small dinner plate
Sheet of construction paper
Pencil
Scissors

Tape
String
Large wooden bead*

*Available at craft stores.

Directions:

1. Lay the plate upside down on the construction paper, and trace around it. Cut out the circle. Then cut from the edge of the circle to the center.

2. Wrap the circle into a cone shape. Tape it closed.

3. Knot 1 end of the string. Thread the other end down through the hole in the bottom of the cone.

4. Thread the unknotted end of the string through the bead. Tie several knots so the bead won't fall off.

5. To play with your bilboquet, hold the cone and let the ball hang down. Swing the ball into the air and try to catch it in the cone.

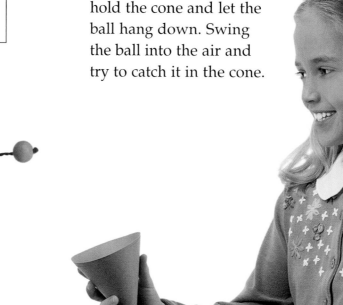

Stenciled Place Mats

Tape a stencil to a canvas place mat with masking tape. If you are using more than one color of paint, tape off the areas of the stencil that will be a different color. Use a sponge to lightly paint the open areas. Let the paint dry. To add a second color, remove the tape from the covered areas of the stencil, and tape over the areas that are already painted.

Papyrotamia (pap-uh-roh-TAY-mee-uh)

You will need:

2 pieces of construction paper in different colors
Pencil
Tracing paper

Tape
Scissors
Glue

*In colonial times, paper was expensive and scarce. On special occasions, people cut paper into decorative designs to give as gifts. This craft was called **papyrotamia**.*

Directions:

1. Fold 1 sheet of construction paper in half. Set it aside.

2. Trace a pattern from page 80 onto tracing paper. Tape the pattern to the construction paper. Be sure the dotted line is on the fold of the construction paper.

3. Cut through the tracing paper pattern and construction paper along the pattern lines. Remove the pattern and tape.

4. Unfold the design. Glue it onto the other piece of construction paper to make a card or anything else you wish.

step 2

step 3

step 4

Felicity's New Year's Ball

Ring in the New Year with dining and dancing.

Miss Sarah Mayer presents her compliments to Miss Michelle Andrews and requests the favor of her attendance at Felicity's New Year's Ball at 356 Hill Avenue on Saturday, January 3rd at 6:00 in the evening.

Fan Invitation

For each invitation, trace the fan pattern from page 79. Tape the pattern to a piece of light-colored paper. Cut it out. Write the invitation on one side of the fan. Then decorate both sides. Fold the fan and tie a ribbon around it. Copy the fancy letters and numbers on page 78 if you like.

Decorations

Look around your neighborhood and backyard for evergreens, holly, and pinecones to decorate for your party. Tie them together with ribbons, and arrange them on your tables.

Minuet

Grace is the key for this "queen of dances"!

1. Stand next to your partner and hold hands. Both of you walk forward—left, right, left. Point your right toes. Walk forward again, starting with your right feet.

2. Face your partner and hold hands. Step on your left feet and swing your right feet forward. Step on your right feet and swing your left feet forward.

3. One partner lets go with her right hand, raises her left arm, and twirls her partner under her arm.

4. Repeat steps 1 to 3. Once you have the steps down, repeat them to music. Look for recordings of classical music by Bach or Mozart at your library.

Twelfth Night Cake

Twelfth Night was celebrated with a special cake. It usually had smooth white icing and was decorated with colorful candied flowers and fruits. Make your favorite cake recipe. Just before you put the batter in the oven, drop in a dried bean. Bake the cake according to the directions. Once it has cooled, add icing and candy decorations. The person who finds the bean is the queen of the feast!

TWELFTH NIGHT

Colonists in Virginia celebrated the holiday season from mid-December until January 6, or Twelfth Night. Twelfth Night is a celebration based on a Bible story about the arrival of the Three Wise Men in Bethlehem, 12 days after Christmas. In colonial times, Twelfth Night was often celebrated with a fancy meal and a ball.

Eggnog

Gently heat a quart of eggnog in a saucepan, stirring just until warm. Pour it into a punch bowl, sprinkle nutmeg on top, and place it on a pretty party table with cups for everyone.

New Year's Cookies

In colonial times, these cookies were made to celebrate the New Year. Use your favorite sugar cookie dough or a tube of refrigerated cookie dough. Roll out the dough, and then use cookie cutters to cut out shapes. In a small bowl, mix 2 teaspoons of nutmeg and 2 tablespoons of sugar. Sprinkle the sugar mixture on the cookies. Bake them according to the directions.

Felicity's Plantation Picnic

*Summertime was perfect for a plantation picnic.
Have one of your own!*

Sweet-Smelling Invitation

Write out each invitation on a small card. Put
it in an envelope and sprinkle dried potpourri
inside. Or punch a hole in the card, thread a
ribbon through it, and tie the ribbon around
a flower. Deliver your invitations the old-
fashioned way—by hand!

Lemon Tartlets

Follow the directions to bake pre-made
miniature pastry shells. Spoon lemon curd*
into the shells. Refrigerate them until it's time
for the party. Top with raspberries, blueberries,
and a sprinkling of powdered sugar.

Available at most supermarkets.

Chicken Salad

Chop 2 celery ribs and 4 hard-boiled eggs.
Combine the celery, eggs, and 4 cups cooked
or canned chicken in a mixing bowl. In a small
bowl, mix $1/3$ cup mayonnaise, 1 teaspoon
Dijon mustard, 1 teaspoon dried tarragon,
and salt and pepper to taste. Mix well. Add
the dressing to the chicken. Refrigerate it
until it's time to eat. Serve it on
sandwiches or scooped on
a bed of lettuce.

Cranberry-Apple Punch

Mix together 2 quarts of
cranberry juice, 1 pint of apple
juice, and 1 pint of lemonade. Pour the
punch into a pretty pitcher, add ice, and
it's ready to serve.

Quoits

For this game you will need 2 wooden dowels for the *hobs*, or pins, and 8 small embroidery hoops for the *quoits*, or rings. Paint a dowel and 4 hoops one color, and the other dowel and hoops another color. To play, push a hob into the ground. Push another hob into the ground 10 feet from the first. The players divide into 2 teams. Each team chooses a color and stands by a hob. Team A tosses their quoits to the other team's hob. Then Team B tosses their quoits. Teams get a point for every quoit that rings the hob. Play up to 10 points.

These girls from 1896 are playing quoits, just as Felicity might have.

Bowls

Divide your guests into 2 teams. Each team gets 4 *bowls*, or balls, such as croquet balls. Throw a *jack*, or target ball, onto the lawn. The teams stand at a starting line and take turns throwing their bowls as close to the jack as they can. The team with the bowl closest to the jack wins.

BATTLEDORE AND SHUTTLECOCK

In colonial days, badminton was called "battledore and shuttlecock." If colonial children didn't have a battledore, or racket, they used their school hornbooks as rackets! Felicity might have said this rhyme as she played. Say a line with each swing, and keep repeating it until the shuttlecock falls.

One, two, three, four,
Mary at the cottage door,
Eating cherries off a plate,
Five, six, seven, eight.

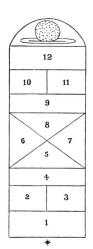

Scotch-Hoppers

Felicity called hopscotch "scotch-hoppers." Use chalk to draw this colonial hopscotch pattern on the sidewalk or driveway. Take turns tossing a stone and hopping to the top!

Josefina's New M...

Create a colorful celebration f...

In 1824, New Mexicans celebrated religious holidays and special occasions such as weddings, baptisms, or the arrival of guests. The celebrations were filled with friends and family, and the whole village was welcome. Everyone gathered for good food, singing, storytelling, and guitar and fiddle music.

Charlotte

Miss Gabrielle Anderson
requests the honor
of your presence
at Josefina's
New Mexican Party
at 36 Owen Drive
on Saturday, May 20,
at 2:00

ican Party

ur friends!

Ramillete Invitation

A *ramillete (rah-mee-YEH-teh)* is a decorative paper flower. Making a ramillete is like making a paper snowflake. Place a drinking glass on colored paper, trace around it, and cut out the circle. Fold it in half at least 3 times to make a wedge shape. Cut shapes into each side of the wedge. Unfold it, and you'll see the flower. Make other ramilletes in different sizes. Use them to decorate a round basic card (see pattern on page 84).

Framed Name Cards

Decorate a name card with colors Josefina might have used. Follow the design shown or make up your own. Use crayons, markers, or paints.

19

New Mexican Treats

Josefina's table was set with colorful dishes and pottery.
Fill bowls and plates with these delicious sweets!

This caramel custard is a traditional Spanish dessert. Decorate it with mint leaves if you like.

Flan

You will need:

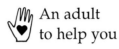 An adult to help you

Ingredients:
1 cup sugar
2 tablespoons water
8 eggs, beaten
2 cups sugar
1/2 teaspoon salt
4 cups milk
1 teaspoon vanilla

Equipment:
Measuring cups
   and spoons
2 saucepans
2 wooden spoons
6 1/2-inch baking dish
Mixing bowl
Deep baking pan
Potholders

Directions:

1. Preheat the oven to 325°. Put 1 cup of sugar in a saucepan. Set the pan over high heat and stir constantly. The sugar should be completely melted and a deep rich brown.

2. Have an adult add the water carefully—it may splatter. Mix well. Pour into the baking dish.

step 2

3. In a mixing bowl, stir together the eggs, 2 cups of sugar, and the salt.

4. Pour the milk in a saucepan. Have an adult heat it on medium-high, stirring constantly, until just boiling.

5. Stir 6 tablespoons of the hot milk into the egg mixture. Then pour the egg mixture into the milk and mix well. Add the vanilla. Pour the mixture into the baking dish.

6. Place the dish in the baking pan. Fill the pan with hot water halfway up the side of the dish. Bake for 1 hour or until the custard is set. Refrigerate at least 3 hours. Then have an adult turn the flan upside down onto a plate to serve.

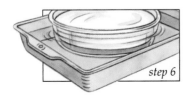
step 6

Bizcochitos (bees-ko-CHEE-tohs)

You will need:

An adult to help you

Ingredients:
2 cups flour
1 cup lard
1³/4 cups sugar
3 eggs, beaten
2 tablespoons anise seed
2 tablespoons vanilla
4 tablespoons water
Cinnamon and sugar
  for topping

Equipment:
Measuring cups
  and spoons
Mixing bowl
Pastry cutter
Mixing spoon
Rolling pin
Cookie cutters
Spatula
2 cookie sheets
Small bowl
Pastry brush
Potholders

These tender cookies melt in your mouth!

Directions:

1. Preheat the oven to 375°. Put the flour in a mixing bowl.

2. Use a pastry cutter to cut the lard into the flour. Add the sugar, eggs, and anise seed. Mix well.

step 2

3. Form the mixture into a firm dough. Add more flour if you need to. Flour the counter and roll out the dough until it is ¹/4 inch thick.

step 3

4. Use the cookie cutters to cut out the dough. With the spatula, place the cookies on a cookie sheet.

step 4

5. In the small bowl, combine the vanilla and water. Brush it on the tops of the cookies. Sprinkle with cinnamon and sugar.

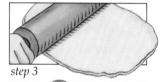
step 5

6. Bake the cookies for 3 to 5 minutes or until slightly brown. Serve warm.

Lemonade

Roll 6 lemons on the table to loosen the juice. Cut the lemons in half and squeeze the juice out. In a pitcher, stir together the lemon juice, 1 cup of sugar, and 8 cups of cold water. Chill it until you're ready to serve. Serve with lemon slices and sprigs of mint.

Spanish Songs and Games

Josefina and her sisters played these games.

El florón (el flo-ROHN), or The Flower

One player is the Guesser. The other players sit in a circle holding their closed fists out in front of them. The Guesser closes her eyes. One of the players hides the *florón*—a flower blossom or other small object—in her hand. Then players chant the lines below as the Guesser tries to guess who has the florón. If the Guesser is correct, she and the hider switch places.

> *The flower goes in the hands,*
> *And in the hands it has spoken.*
> *Guess who has it, guess who has it,*
> *Or be taken for a fool!*

WHAT AM I?

New Mexican children had to work hard, but they found time to have fun, too. During work and play they told riddles and stories and sang songs. See if you can guess this riddle from Josefina's time.

> *Although I have feet, I can't move myself;*
> *I carry the meal on my top and can't eat it.*

Answer: A table.

The Rainbow

Players choose a home base. One player is the Angel. The other players are the Rainbow. They each think of a color to be—without saying their color out loud. Then the Angel calls out a color. When a player's color is named, she runs for the base while the Angel tries to catch her. If she reaches the base before the Angel, she chooses another color and rejoins the rainbow. If the Angel catches her, that player is out of the game.

The Sea Serpent

This game is much like London Bridge. Two players hold their hands up high to form a bridge. The other players form a line, each holding onto the waist of the player in front of her. The line weaves under the bridge like a sea serpent as the players chant the lines below. At the next-to-last line, the players forming a bridge drop their arms to catch a player. Gently, they rock her back and forth. Then the game starts again.

The sea serpent we like to play
To have fun, to have fun.
Under the bridge all on a track,
Children in front go faster and faster.
If you don't follow, you'll stay back,
Back, back, back, back.

The Coyote and the Fox

Choose 2 leaders, the Coyote and the Fox. Everyone but the Coyote lines up behind the Fox. Each player holds the waist of the girl in front of her to form a chain. Then the Fox and the chain circle around the Coyote. The Coyote must try to catch a girl in the chain. The chain circles and twists around trying to get away from the Coyote. When a girl is caught, she becomes the Coyote and the Coyote becomes the Fox.

The Little Burro

This game is similar to leapfrog. All the players stand in a line and pretend to ride burros as they chant:

Hurry, my little burro,
Hurry, hurry, hurry,
Carry me as we trot,
Hurry, hurry, hurry,
Carry me as we gallop.
Hurry up, hurry up.

Then the players crouch down. The last player in line leaps over everyone until she is at the front. Keep leaping until everyone has had a chance. Then the game starts again.

Beautiful Blossoms

These flowery crafts are lots of fun!

Plant a primrose or another favorite flower in this pretty pot.

Majolica (ma-JAH-la-ka) Pot

You will need:

An adult to help you
Wax paper or an old plastic tablecloth
Disposable thin plastic gloves
Spray can of clear sealer*
Clay flowerpots and saucers

Pencils
Brushes of different sizes
Acrylic paints in different colors
Clear acrylic spray*

*Available at paint or hardware stores.

Before the party:

1. Cover your work surface with wax paper or an old plastic tablecloth. Put on gloves. With an adult, carefully read the directions on the sealer can.

step 1

2. Working with an adult, spray the flowerpots and saucers with sealer. Let them sit for about 30 minutes, or until they are totally dry. Then apply a second coat and let it dry.

step 2

At the party:

3. Have your guests use the pencils to draw designs on the flowerpots. Then paint the pots using any colors you wish.

step 3

4. Let the pots dry. Then ask an adult to spray the outsides of the pots with clear acrylic spray, following the directions on the can.

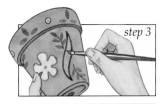

step 4

5. Let the pots dry. At home, each guest can plant herbs or a flower in her pot.

Cornhusk Flowers

You will need:

An adult to help you
Large pot
Fabric dye, various colors
1/2 gallon of water
Dry cornhusks
Paper towels
Fine spool wire
Scissors
Cloth-covered stem wire
Floral tape

Brighten up your room with colorful cornhusks.

Before the party:

1. Ask an adult to help you. In the large pot, dissolve half a package of fabric dye in the water. Heat the mixture to boiling. Put the husks in the dye, and then take the pot off the heat. Let the husks soak overnight or until they are the shade you want. Pat them dry with paper towels. Repeat with as many colors of dye as you like.

At the party:

2. Tear the husks into 2-inch-wide strips. Make the center of the flower by rolling 3 or 4 strips together. Wrap wire around them about 1 inch from the end.

3. Fold a strip in half to make a petal. Position it against the center. Wrap wire around it, twist the ends together, and trim off the wire ends. Add other petals around the center in the same way.

4. Cut the extra husks on the bottom of the flower into a point.

5. Cut a piece of stem wire 18 inches long. Bend 1 end into a hook. Insert the other end into the center of the flower from above and pull it all the way in, until the hook disappears into the flower.

6. Wrap floral tape around the base of the flower and all the way down the stem. Pull it tight so it sticks to itself.

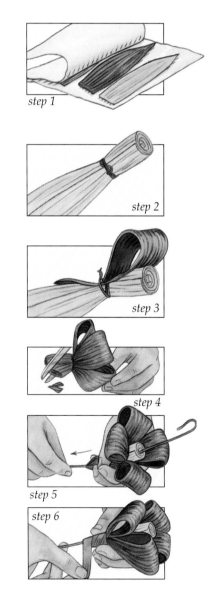

step 1

step 2

step 3

step 4

step 5

step 6

Josefina's Harvest Celebration

In New Mexico, the harvest was a time to gather together.
Gather your own friends for a harvest celebration!

Corn Invitation

For each invitation, trace the corn patterns from pages 80–81. Tape the patterns to construction paper and cut them out. Glue the 2 husks together around the edges. They should make a pocket. Decorate the front of the corncob and write your invitation on the back. Slide the corncob into the husk pocket.

Husk the Corn and come to Josefina's Harvest Celebration!

Miss Lucy Adams requests the honor of your presence at Josefina's Harvest Celebration at 481 Lark Lane on Saturday, September 27, at 4:00

THE HARVEST

*At harvest time, families and neighbors prepared food to be stored through the winter. The women and girls gathered in the **placita**, or courtyard, to husk and roast corn and prepare fruits and vegetables. As they worked, they sang and told stories.*

Illustration by Jean-Paul Tibbles from *Meet Josefina*.

The Little Blind Hen

One player is the Hen. She is blindfolded and spun around 3 times. The other players join hands and circle around the Hen. They call out, "Little Blind Hen, what are you doing?"

Little Blind Hen: "I am looking for some grains of corn."
Players: "What are they for?"
Little Blind Hen: "They are for my little chicks."
Players: "Pray give us one grain."
Little Blind Hen: "No!"
Players: "May you lose them then!"

Then the hen reaches out and tries to touch a player. When she does, they switch places.

Empanaditas *(em-pah-nah-DEE-tahs)*

You will need:

 An adult to help you

Ingredients:

For the turnovers:
2 cups flour
2 teaspoons baking powder
2 tablespoons sugar
1 teaspoon salt
$\frac{1}{2}$ cup shortening
$\frac{1}{3}$ cup ice water
Cinnamon applesauce or jam

For the topping:
1 cup sugar
1 tablespoon cinnamon

Equipment:
Mixing bowl
Measuring cups and spoons
Wooden spoon
Pastry cutter
Rolling pin
Round cookie cutter
Spoon
Fork
Spatula
Cookie sheet
Potholders
Small bowl

Fill these sweet, bite-size pastry pockets with your favorite applesauce or jam.

Directions:

1. Preheat the oven to 400°. In a mixing bowl, mix the flour, baking powder, sugar, and salt. Use the pastry cutter to cut the shortening into the flour mixture.

2. Add enough ice water to hold the dough together. Roll the dough out on a floured counter. Use a round cookie cutter to cut out circles.

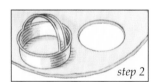
step 2

3. Place a spoonful of applesauce or jam on each circle. Fold the circles over and press the edges firmly together with a fork.

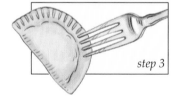
step 3

4. Place turnovers on a cookie sheet and bake for 15 to 20 minutes, or until golden. Remove from oven.

5. In a small bowl, mix the sugar and cinnamon. While the turnovers are still warm, carefully dip them in the mixture. Let cool.

step 5

Roasted Pine Nuts

In a skillet, warm 1 tablespoon each of butter and sugar over medium heat. Stir in $\frac{3}{4}$ cup of pine nuts. Add 1 to $1\frac{1}{2}$ tablespoons ground dried mild chile. Continue stirring to coat well until the nuts begin to crackle. Pour them onto a baking sheet to cool.

Josefina's Fandango

Invite your friends to an evening filled with music, dance, and laughter.

Dancing Slippers Invitation

For each invitation, trace the patterns from pages 82–83. Tape the patterns to construction paper and cut them out. Write your invitation on the insoles of the slippers. Glue them to the slippers. Then glue bows on the toes.

Come dance at Josefina's Fandango!

Miss Lily Schulze requests the honor of your presence at Josefina's Fandango at 657 Sage Court on Saturday, December 15, at 6:00.

Decorations

Farolitos (fah-ro-LEE-tohs) are a modern version of *luminarias* (loo-mee-NAH-ree-ahs), or bonfires. Set small paper bags along your walkway. Put sand and a votive candle in the bottom of each bag. Ask an adult to light them for you.

Waltz of the Broom

This dance is a bit like musical chairs. Look for recordings of Spanish folk music at your library. An odd number of dancers form 2 lines facing each other. Start the music. The dancer without a partner dances between the lines with a broom. Suddenly, she drops her broom and grabs a partner. Then everyone grabs a partner. The dancer without one is the new broom dancer.

THE FANDANGO

*A **fandango** (fahn-DAHN-go) is a party that includes lively dancing. In Josefina's time, a fandango was part of many special occasions, such as weddings, religious feast days, and the arrival of visitors from far away. A fandango was held in the **gran sala**, or biggest room, of the house. Musicians played at one end of the room, the food was at the other end, and the middle of the room was for dancing.*

New Mexican Hot Chocolate

In a saucepan, combine 6 ounces sweet cooking chocolate, 6 cups milk, 2 teaspoons cinnamon, and 2 teaspoons sugar. Cook the mixture over low heat. Stir it constantly until the chocolate melts and the mixture is blended. Just before serving, use an egg beater and beat until frothy. Add a cinnamon stick stirrer, if you wish.

Marquesote (mahr-keh-SO-teh), or Sponge Cake

Make or buy a sponge cake. Decorate it with apricots and apricot jam.

Anise Cakes

You will need:

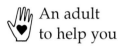 An adult to help you

Ingredients:
1/2 cup butter, softened
1 1/2 cups sugar
3 eggs
1 teaspoon anise seed
3 cups flour
Almonds

Equipment:
Measuring cups
   and spoons
Mixing bowl
Wooden spoon
Teaspoon
Greased cookie
   sheet
Potholders

Directions:

1. Preheat the oven to 350°. In a mixing bowl, cream the butter and sugar. Add the eggs, 1 at a time. Beat hard after each addition.

2. Stir in the anise seed and flour. Mix well.

3. Drop the batter from a teaspoon onto the cookie sheet. Place an almond on top of each cookie.

4. Bake the cookies for 10 to 12 minutes, or until the bottoms are golden brown and the tops are pale. Remove from the oven and let cool.

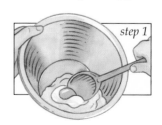
step 1

step 3

Kirsten's Prai

This pioneer party is

An important occasion for pioneers was a bee, or work-play party. Everyone in the area came to help a neighboring family with jobs that were impossible for one family to do alone, like building a house or a barn. When the work was done, everyone ate a huge supper—so they'd have lots of energy for dancing!

Angela

You are respectfully invited to attend Kirsten's Prairie Party at Jane's house 485 Robin Lane on Saturday, June 17 at 3:00.

e Party

y!

GETTING STARTED

Bonnet Invitation

For each invitation, fold a 9-by-12-inch piece of construction paper in half to make a card. Trace the bonnet pattern from page 85. Tape it to the construction paper, and then cut it out. Write the invitation on the inside and decorate the outside. Punch a hole through the card and tie it closed with a ribbon.

Hay Bale Name Cards

Purchase tiny bales of hay from a craft store. Write your guests' names on small cards and slide them into the bales of hay.

Catherine

Music

Pioneer bees usually ended in square dancing, reels, or jigs. A local musician would play lively fiddle music like "Buffalo Gals" or "Old Dan Tucker." Look for square dance music at your library.

Frontier Foods

Most pioneers did not have enough dishes to serve a large group. Set out unmatched plates, cups, and eating utensils. They will make a colorful table!

These lemony teacakes were sweet snacks on the prairie.

Prairie Teacakes

You will need:

 An adult to help you

Ingredients:
1/2 cup butter, softened
1 cup sugar
1 egg
1 tablespoon grated lemon rind
1/2 teaspoon lemon extract
2 cups flour
2 teaspoons baking powder
1 cup milk
Butter to grease the pan
Lemon glaze (see below)

Equipment:
2 mixing bowls
Measuring cups and spoons
Wooden spoon
Paper towel
Muffin pan
Potholders

Directions:

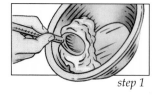
step 1

1. Preheat the oven to 350°. In a mixing bowl, cream the butter and sugar. Add the egg, lemon rind, and lemon extract to the mixture. Stir well.

2. In a separate bowl, mix together the flour and the baking powder. Add the flour mixture to the butter mixture. Add the milk and stir well.

step 3

3. Use a paper towel to grease the pan with butter. Pour the batter into the muffin cups. Bake for 35 to 40 minutes, or until golden. Remove from the oven and let cool. Drizzle lemon glaze on the cakes before serving.

Lemon Glaze

In a small bowl, mix 3/4 cup powdered sugar, 1 teaspoon lemon juice, and 1 teaspoon water. Mix well. If the glaze is too thick to drizzle, add a little more water.

Maple Gingerbread

Preheat the oven to 350°. In a mixing bowl, beat 1 egg. Stir in:

- 1 cup maple syrup
- 1 cup sour cream
- 4 tablespoons melted butter

Add:

- $2^1/_3$ cups flour
- 1 teaspoon baking soda
- $1^1/_2$ teaspoons powdered ginger
- $^1/_2$ teaspoon salt

Mix well. Butter a round baking pan and coat it with flour. Pour the batter into the pan. Bake the cake for 30 minutes or until it pulls away from the pan. When the cake has cooled, frost it with lemon glaze (opposite page) and add candied ginger, if you like.

Ginger Punch

Have an adult help you chop $^1/_4$ pound gingerroot*. Put 1 quart cold water and $^1/_2$ cup sugar in a saucepan. Add the gingerroot. Boil the mixture for 5 minutes. Add 1 cup orange juice and $^1/_2$ cup lemon juice. Cool the mixture and strain out the root. Serve it over ice.

Available at most supermarkets.

Apple Tarts

Core and slice 3 apples into small, thin pieces. In a mixing bowl, combine:

- Apple slices
- $^1/_4$ cup brown sugar
- $^1/_4$ cup flour

Mix well. Partially bake pre-made pastry cups according to the directions. Spoon the mixture into the pastry cups. Place them on a baking sheet and bake at 350° for 15 minutes. Have an adult pour 1 tablespoon cream over each tart. Continue to bake them about 10 more minutes or until the apples are tender. Sprinkle with nutmeg and serve warm.

MAPLE SUGAR

Native Americans taught the pioneers how to tap sugar maple trees to get sap. The pioneers boiled the sap down into syrup and sugar to use for baking. They also made maple sugar candy in these decorative wooden molds.

Maple sugar molds

Frontier Fun

Kirsten played games that featured things she saw around her farm every day—baskets, barn cats, and honey pots.

Jackstraws

Kirsten liked this game, which you know as Pick-up Sticks! Use straws, twigs, or pieces of raw spaghetti as jackstraws. Hold about 10 jackstraws in one hand and let them fall into a loose pile on the floor or table. The first player tries to pick up a jackstraw from the pile without jiggling any other straw. If she touches or moves any others, she loses her turn. If she succeeds in picking up her straw, she gets another turn. When there are no more jackstraws left in the pile, each player counts the number she's picked up. The player with the most jackstraws wins.

Puss in the Corner

To play, you'll need 5 players. Four people make a square, with one person at each corner. The fifth person stands in the middle. She is Puss— she wants a corner too! The object of the game is to change places without letting Puss get a corner. When Puss yells "Change!" all the players scramble to change corners. As they change, Puss tries to run to an empty corner. Whoever is left without a corner becomes Puss.

Here I Bake, Here I Brew

All the players but one join hands to form a circle. That player is held prisoner in the middle. She touches a pair of joined hands in the circle and says, "Here I bake." Then she touches another pair of hands and says, "Here I brew." Suddenly she tries to force her way out of the circle at another spot as she says, "Here I mean to break through!" If she succeeds, she picks a new player to be the prisoner.

I Have a Basket

All the players stand in a circle. The first player begins the game by saying, "I have a basket." The  player beside her asks, "What's inside?" The first player names something that starts with the letter A. The second player then names something that starts with B, and so on. If a player can't think of an object, she sits down. The last person standing is the winner.

Honey Pot

The Honey Pot sits with her knees tucked up to her chest. Two other players pick her up and carry her singing, "Who will buy a Honey Pot?" Then the Honey Pot is passed around to other buyers. If the Honey Pot lets her feet touch the ground, she has to pay a penalty, like singing a silly song. If the carriers drop the Honey Pot, they have to pay the penalty.

Fox and Geese

Draw a huge wagon wheel on the ground. First make a circle about 25 feet wide. Then make 8 spokes across it. One player is the Fox. She chases the other players—the Geese—up and down the spokes and around the outside rim of the circle. When a Goose is tagged, she becomes the Fox.

YOU'RE IT!

Pioneer children chanted counting-out rhymes to decide who would be "it." Try this one:

*Intry, mintry, cutry, corn,
Briar seeds and apple thorns,
Briar, wire, limber lock,
Five geese in a flock,
Sit and sing,
By the spring,
O-u-t and in again.*

Pioneer Playthings

You and your friends can make your own toys, just as Kirsten did.

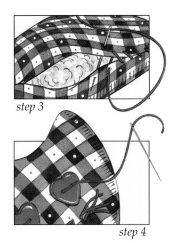

These kittens are as cute as buttons!

Calico Kitten

You will need:

Pencil	Needle
Tracing paper	Thread
Straight pins	Cotton stuffing
Calico fabric, 2 squares,	Fabric glue
8 by 8 inches each	Yarn
Scissors	2 buttons

Directions:

1. Trace the pattern from page 86 onto tracing paper. Pin the paper pattern to 2 layers of calico fabric. Make sure the *right sides,* or pattern sides, of the fabric are facing each other.

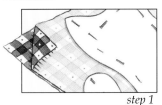

step 1

2. Cut out the kitten. Pin the pieces of fabric together with the right sides facing each other. Use the backstitch on page 5 to sew around the kitten about ¼ inch from the edge. Leave a 2-inch gap open at the bottom of the kitten.

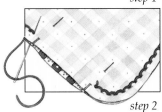

step 2

3. Turn the kitten right-side out. Use a pencil to push out the tail and any narrow points. Stuff the kitten with the cotton. Tuck the raw edges of fabric inside the kitten, and use the whipstitch on page 5 to sew up the gap.

step 3

4. Glue on a yarn mouth and whiskers, or have an adult help you stitch them. Glue or sew on buttons for eyes.

step 4

Straw Horse

You will need:

Loose straw*
Baking pan
Warm water
Paper towels
Scissors
Ruler
Colored yarn

Craft glue
Seed heads* for
  mane and tail
Straight pins
Piece of Styrofoam

Available at craft stores.

Directions:

1. Soak the straw in warm water in the baking pan. After a few minutes, drain the straw and pat it dry with paper towels.

2. Cut 8 pieces of straw so they are 8 inches long. Tightly tie 2 pieces of yarn around the straw bundle, dividing it into equal thirds.

3. To make the front of the horse, bend down 6 straws for the legs. Tie a piece of yarn around 3 of the straws for 1 leg. Do the same for the other leg.

4. Bend up the other 2 straws to make the neck and head. Tie the nose together with an 8-inch piece of yarn. Tie the yarn ends together to make reins. Glue a seed head to the neck for a mane.

5. In the back, bend down all the straws. Tie 4 straws together for each leg. Slide the stem of a seed head into the body for a tail.

6. To help your horse keep its shape, pin the legs into position on a piece of Styrofoam and let it sit overnight.

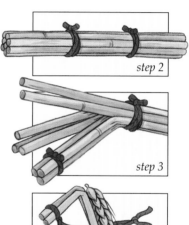

step 2

step 3

step 4

step 5

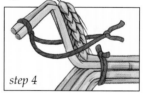

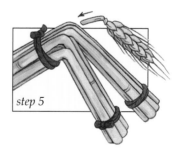

Kirsten might have spent an afternoon making straw horses in the hayloft.

Kirsten's Barn Dance

Plan an evening of pioneer toe-tapping!

Barn Invitation

For each invitation, you will need a 9-by-6-inch piece of red construction paper. Fold the short sides in so they meet in the middle. Cut off the corners to make the roof of the barn. Decorate the outside like a barn and write the invitation on the inside.

Old Dan Tucker

● = *Partner on the right*   ■ = *Partner on the left*   **X** = *Old Dan Tucker*

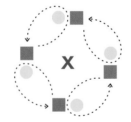
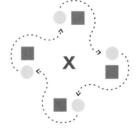
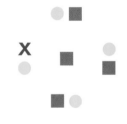

1. All the dancers find a partner and form a circle. The person in the center is Old Dan Tucker. Start the music!

2. Everyone walks forward 4 steps and back 4 steps. Partners on the left shake hands with the person to their left. Then they walk around her and back to their partner.

3. Partners shake hands. Partners on the right walk behind their partner and in front of the next partner. Keep weaving through the circle, clapping to the music.

4. When the music stops, everyone grabs a partner. Old Dan Tucker tries to get in the circle. The person without a partner is now Old Dan Tucker.

Harmonica

Fold a piece of waxed paper so it fits over a small comb. The open end should be on the teeth side. Press your lips lightly against the paper, and hum. Move the comb back and forth to make different sounds.

Baked Apple Dumplings

Mix together 1/2 cup sour cream, 1/2 cup brown sugar, 1/2 cup dried cranberries, and 1/2 table-spoon grated orange rind. Have an adult help you core 6 apples. Fill them with the mixture. Cover the apples with pieces of pre-made piecrust. Use any extra dough to make leaves. Brush the apples with milk and sprinkle them with sugar. Prick them with a fork. Set the apples on a baking sheet and bake at 425° for 30 minutes. Serve warm.

Corn Bread

Make your favorite corn bread. Cut it into pieces and set it in a bowl on the party table. For a sweet spread, make honey butter. Let 1 stick of butter soften, then add 1/4 cup of honey. Whip them together with a fork.

Apple Cider

Have an adult help you pour 4 quarts apple cider into a soup pot. Add 3 cinnamon sticks and 3/4 cup sugar. Heat the mixture over medium-high heat until it *boils*, or bubbles rapidly. Cover the pot and let the mixture *simmer*, or bubble gently, on low heat for 30 minutes. Strain the cider into a pitcher. Serve it hot or cold.

Snap Apple

Tie a string onto an apple stem. Have one person stand on a stool or chair. She swings the string with the apple in front of another player. Without using her hands, the player tries to bite the apple as it swings by.

Apple Dance

Players choose a partner. The couples try to dance for a whole song with an apple pressed between their foreheads.

Kirsten's Patchwork Party

Trade stories with your friends at a pioneer sewing bee.

Patchwork Invitation

Fold a 6-by-12-inch piece of construction paper in half to make a card. Make a quilt square on the front with squares of patterned paper cut with pinking shears. Inside, write your invitation.

Cat's Cradle

1. Tie a 6-foot piece of string into a loop, and place the loop over your hands as shown.

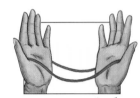
step 1

2. Dip 1 hand over and then under the string so it wraps around the top of your palm. Repeat with the other hand.

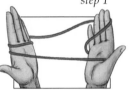
step 2

3. With your middle finger, pick up the string lying across the opposite palm. Repeat with the other hand.

step 3

4. Now you have a cradle! See what other shapes you can make.

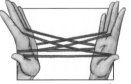
step 4

Handkerchief Doll

Cut a 6-inch circle of light-colored fabric. Wrap the circle around a ball of stuffing, and tie it with a string. This is the head. Fold a handkerchief or a 15-by-15-inch square of fabric in half so it makes a triangle. One point should be at the top. Place the head at the top point of the handkerchief. Roll the 2 side points in so they meet in the center. These are the legs. Tie the handkerchief closed under the doll's neck. Draw on a face if you like.

Patchwork Cake

Bake an 8-inch-square chocolate cake, white cake, and yellow cake. Frost the top of each a different color. Cut each cake into 9 equal squares. Arrange them on a plate so they form a patchwork, then frost the sides of the cake. Decorate with colorful candy buttons.

Quilt Square Cookies

Make your favorite sugar cookie dough or use refrigerated cookie dough. Roll out the dough, cut it into squares, and bake. Frost the cookies with white frosting. Have each guest decorate her own square with decorator icing and candies. Place them together on a tray so they form a friendship quilt.

Spiced Chocolate

Have an adult help you slowly heat 1 quart of milk in a saucepan. Stir it constantly until it boils. Put in 1 cinnamon stick and $\frac{1}{3}$ cup chocolate chips. Let the mixture boil quickly, and turn off the heat. When it cools a bit, ask an adult to pour it into party mugs and sprinkle nutmeg on the top. Add whipped cream for a frothy final touch!

QUILTING BEES

*Quilting parties, or **bees,** gave girls and women a chance to get together with their friends. While they sewed, they traded stories and shared news. When they finished a quilt, they liked to test its strength. They would try to push an unsuspecting person into the quilt and toss her high into the air. A good quilt would hold the weight of a person. If it didn't, they knew they had been too busy trading stories!*

Addy's Freed

Gather friends for an emancipat

During Addy's time, people had parties to celebrate freedom from slavery. The first emancipation celebration was on December 31, 1862, when people waited up all night to hear President Lincoln's Emancipation Proclamation. Have your Freedom Party anytime you like.

Pam

In 1865
Addy became free.

Come celebrate
her joy with me!

n Party

bration!

Caroline

GETTING STARTED

Banner Invitation

Cut a 4-by-
8-inch piece
of red paper and a
6-by-2½-inch piece of
white paper. Glue the
white paper in the center
of the red paper. Fold the
invitation in half. Fold the
top layer back in half
again. Unfold the paper,
and then write the invitation. Decorate with stars.

Lantern Name Cards

Fold a 4½-by-6-inch piece
of construction paper in
half lengthwise. Cut slits
along the fold
line, about
½ inch
apart. Unfold the
paper and glue it into
a ring. Push it down a bit
so it makes a lantern
shape. Write your guest's
name on it.

Tissue Paper Flowers

Stack eight 6-by-6-
inch pieces of tissue
paper. Pleat them,
accordion-style.
Fasten the pleat-
ed tissues in the
middle with florist's wire.
Pull up the "petals" carefully, and arrange them
into a pretty flower.

Scrumptious Sweets

These tasty treats were Addy's favorites!

Bundle your benne candy in pieces of cellophane, and then tie them with colorful cord.

Benne (BEN-ee) Candy

You will need:

An adult to help you

Ingredients:
2 cups sugar
½ teaspoon vanilla extract
½ teaspoon lemon extract
1 cup lightly toasted sesame seeds

Equipment:
Measuring cups and spoons
Saucepan
Wooden spoon
Buttered baking pan
Knife
Potholders

Directions:

1. Measure out the sugar and place it in the saucepan. Add the extracts to the sugar. Set the pan over high heat. Melt the sugar, stirring constantly.

step 2

2. When the sugar is melted, remove it from the heat and add the sesame seeds, stirring quickly. Immediately pour the mixture into the buttered baking pan.

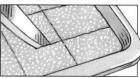
step 3

3. Use the knife to mark 1-inch squares on the mixture while it is still warm. If the knife sticks, run hot water on it. When the candy is cool, turn it out of the pan and break it along the marked lines.

GOOD LUCK SEEDS

*When Africans arrived in America, they introduced **benne**, or sesame, seeds to America. The seeds were a symbol of good luck. Some people planted benne seeds around their homes to bring good luck to everyone who lived there.*

Mini Sweet Potato Pies

You will need:

 An adult to help you

Ingredients:
2 6-oz. jars sweet potato
  baby food
$\frac{1}{4}$ cup melted butter
$\frac{1}{2}$ cup sugar
$\frac{1}{4}$ cup brown sugar
3 eggs
$\frac{1}{2}$ cup evaporated milk
$\frac{1}{2}$ teaspoon nutmeg
$\frac{1}{2}$ teaspoon cinnamon
$\frac{1}{2}$ teaspoon vanilla
Pre-made pastry cups

Equipment:
Measuring cups
  and spoons
Mixing bowl
Wooden spoon
Baking sheet
Butter knife
Potholders

Try sprinkling cinnamon and nutmeg on top of these tiny pies.

Directions:

1. Preheat the oven to 375°. Combine the sweet potatoes and the melted butter in a mixing bowl. Add the sugars and the eggs. Mix until smooth.

2. Add the milk, nutmeg, cinnamon, and vanilla. Beat well. Spoon the batter into the pastry cups.

3. Place the pies on a baking sheet. Bake for 30 minutes or until a knife comes out dry after it is inserted into the center. Have an adult remove the pies from the oven, and let cool.

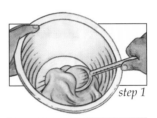
step 1

step 2

Tangy Iced Tea

Have an adult pour 6 cups of boiling water into a large mixing bowl. Hang 6 tea bags over the edge of the bowl, and let the tea steep for 5 minutes. Pour the tea into a pitcher. Add 1 cup each of apple juice, orange juice, and pineapple juice. Add $\frac{1}{2}$ cup sugar, 3 tablespoons lemon juice, and 1 cinnamon stick. Mix well and serve with a fruit wedge.

Fruity Ice Cream

Place raspberries, orange slices, or other fruit in a bowl and sprinkle it with sugar. Let it sit at room temperature for a few hours so a syrup begins to develop. When it's time for the party, serve the fruit and syrup over vanilla ice cream. Yummy!

45

Amusing Activities

Addy and Sarah played these games together.

Ribbon's End

All the players but one stand in a line. Each player puts her hands on the shoulders of the player in front of her. The player not in line is the Catcher. She stands facing the line and tries to catch the Ribbon's End—the last player in the line. The line twists and turns to get away from the Catcher. When she finally catches the Ribbon's End, she becomes the Ribbon's End and the girl in front is the new Catcher.

Feather

All the players sit in a circle. One person starts the game by tossing the feather into the air and blowing on it to keep it floating. Then the other players in the circle join in to try to keep the feather afloat.

Hot Boiled Beans

 One player is sent out of the room, and a small object is hidden. When the player hears "Hot boiled beans and bacon for supper, hurry up before it gets cold," she returns to the room and searches for the hidden object. The rest of the players tell her that her supper is "very cold," "cold," "hot," "very hot," or "burning." The nearer to the object she is, the hotter her supper gets! Once the player finds the hidden object, the game starts again.

Shadow Buff

One player sits facing a blank wall. Another player stands behind her and shines a flashlight or lamp directly toward the wall. Other players walk behind the sitting player so their shadows are cast on the wall. They try to disguise themselves, and the sitting player tries to guess who the shadows are. When she guesses the right player, they switch places.

Little Sally Walker

The players form a ring around one player, who is Sally Walker. The players in the circle chant these lines as Sally acts them out.

Little Sally Walker,
Sitting in a saucer,
Crying and a-weeping
Over all that she has done.

Rise, Sally, rise.
Wipe out your eyes.
Fly to the east, Sally,

Fly to the west, Sally,
Fly to the very one that
you love the best.

Now Miss Sally,
Jump for joy, jump for joy.
And now, Miss Sally,
won't you bow.

THE CHECKERED GAME OF LIFE

When Addy was growing up, the Checkered Game of Life was a popular board game. Players moved their tokens through School, Honor, and Truth to arrive at Happy Old Age. During the Civil War, the game was a favorite with the soldiers. It was put in a package called Games for Soldiers along with chess, checkers, backgammon, and five versions of dominoes.

47

Crafts for Play

These crafts were Addy's favorite toys.

Spool Puppet

You will need:

Scissors
Ruler
Yarn
9 wooden spools*
Beads
String

Unsharpened pencil or
   dowel
Acrylic paints for
   decoration (*optional*)

* Available at most craft stores.

Directions:

1. Cut a 12-inch piece of yarn. Tightly wrap the middle of it around a spool. Tie a knot.

2. Thread both ends of yarn through another spool and a bead. Tie a triple knot. This is the head. The sideways spool is the chest.

3. Thread a 12-inch piece of yarn through the chest spool. Add a spool and a bead to each side. Tie a triple knot at each end. These are the arms.

4. Cut a 40-inch piece of yarn. Tightly wrap the middle of the yarn around the chest until it is covered. You should still have two 8-inch tails of yarn hanging at the bottom of the spool. Tie a knot as close to the chest as possible.

5. Thread the ends through another spool and knot them again. This is the waist.

6. For legs, add 2 spools and a bead to each piece of yarn. Tie a triple knot at each end. Decorate your puppet if you wish.

step 2

step 3

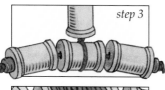

steps 4 and 5

step 6

To make your puppet dance, tie string to the knots at each arm and the head. Tie the other ends around the pencil or dowel.

Bean Doll

You will need:

Tracing paper
Pencil
Scissors
Plain fabric, 10 by 20 inches
Straight pins
Needle
Thread
Cotton stuffing
Dried beans
String

Embroidery floss
  or fabric markers
Ruler or tape measure
Patterned fabric,
  6 by 14 inches
Ribbon
Yarn
Cardboard, 7 by 5 inches
Glue

*Addy named her bean doll Ida Bean because
she was full of beans!*

Directions:

1. Trace the pattern from page 87 onto tracing paper
   and cut it out. Fold the plain fabric in half, and pin
   the pattern to it. Cut out the doll body.

2. Pin the doll shapes together with the *right sides*,
   or front sides, together. Use the directions on
   page 5 to sew a backstitch around the body,
   1/4 inch from the edge. Turn the doll inside out
   through the gap at the bottom.

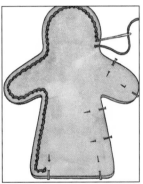

step 2

3. Stuff her head, arms, and neck with the cotton.
   Fill her lower body with beans. Tuck in the raw
   edges and sew up the gap with a whipstitch from
   page 5. Tie string around her neck to give it shape.
   Draw or stitch on a face.

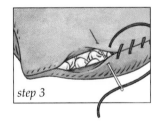

step 3

4. For a simple dress, cut a 2-by-1 1/2-inch hole in
   the center of the patterned fabric. Slip it over her
   head and tie around the waist with a ribbon.

5. For her hair, wrap yarn around the cardboard 30
   times. Slip a short piece of yarn under the
   wrapped yarn and pull it to 1 end. Tie it in a
   double knot and cut off the ends. Cut the yarn
   open at the bottom of the cardboard.

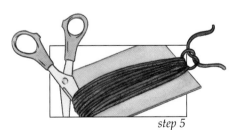

step 5

6. Glue the yarn hair to your doll's head, and style it
   any way you wish.

step 6

Addy's Summer Fair

Excitement is in the air at this fair!

> Miss Abigail Jones hopes to have the pleasure of your company at Addy's Summer Fair at 345 Island Drive on Saturday, June 17 at 1:00.

> Come to Addy's Summer Fair!

Fair Booth Invitation

For each invitation, fold a 9-by-12-inch piece of construction paper in half. Cut off the corners to make the roof of the booth. Decorate the front with pieces of construction paper, rickrack, ribbon, and a toothpick flag. Write the invitation on the inside.

Strawberry Shortcake

Have an adult help you cut the tops off 1 quart of strawberries. Wash them, and then cut them into thin slices. Put the slices into a mixing bowl. Add ½ cup of sugar or to taste and mix well. Spread the strawberries over slices of pound cake or sponge cake, and serve with whipped topping.

Fruit Pies

Unfold pre-made pastry piecrusts. Use a circle cookie cutter or a glass to cut out small circles. Place a spoonful of jam in the center of one of the circles. Put another circle of dough on top. Press the edges together with a wet fork. Repeat for the rest of the circles. Bake at 400° for 15 to 20 minutes or until golden brown.

Lemonade

Roll 6 lemons on the table to loosen the juice. Cut the lemons in half and squeeze out the juice. Stir together the lemon juice, 1 cup of sugar, and 8 cups of cold water in a pitcher. Chill until you're ready to serve.

Juggling Balls

You will need:

(For each ball)
3 balloons
Funnel
3/4 cup dried lentils or peas
Scissors

You'll have a ball juggling these!

Directions:

1. Blow up 1 balloon, hold it for about 30 seconds, and then deflate it. Insert a funnel into the balloon, and pour in the dried lentils or peas. When the balloon is filled, cut off the thick rubber lip.

step 1

2. Cut off the entire neck of a second balloon. Insert 3 fingers from each hand into the second balloon and carefully work it over the first balloon. The 2 neck openings should be at opposite sides.

step 2

3. Cut off the entire neck of a third balloon, and carefully work it over the other 2. Repeat steps 1–3 to make 2 more balls. When you've got 3, you're ready to juggle!

Jump Rope

Girls like Addy chanted these counting rhymes as they jumped.

Wire briar, limberlock,
Three geese in a flock.
One flew east, and one flew west,
And one flew over the cuckoo's nest.
One, two, three…

The clock stands still
While the hands go around.
One o'clock, two o'clock,
Three o'clock…

Addy's Stitch-in-Time Party

Your friends will have SEW much fun at this party!

Make a Spool Card

For each invitation, fold a 9-by-12-inch piece of construction paper in half lengthwise. Trace the spool pattern from page 88. Place the pattern along the folded edge of the card. Tape the pattern in place, and cut out the spool. Wrap yarn around the middle of the front of the card. Write the invitation on the inside.

Pincushion Cupcakes

Follow the directions on a cake mix box to make cupcakes. Frost them with icing, and then use decorator icing and candies to make the cupcakes look like pincushions. Make pins out of toothpicks and colorful gumdrops or jelly beans.

Butterscotch Milk

Have an adult help you slowly heat 1 quart of milk in a saucepan over low heat. Stir constantly until it boils. Add ⅓ cup butterscotch chips. Turn up the heat and let the mixture boil briefly. Turn off the heat. When the milk cools a bit, pour it into mugs. Add a candy stirrer if you like.

Sew Sweets

Make button cookies by decorating plain sugar cookies with decorator icing and candies. Make candy spools with marshmallows and chocolate wafer cookies. Glue them together with frosting, and then paint the marshmallows with a mix of food coloring and water.

Beanbags

You will need:

(For each beanbag)
Fabric, 8 by 5 inches
Straight pins
Needle
Thread
Scissors
Dried beans or peas

These beanbags are easy to make and fun to toss.

Directions:

1. Fold the piece of fabric in half so that it is 4 inches long. Make sure that the right sides of the fabric are facing each other.

2. Pin the fabric, then use the backstitch on page 5 to sew around the square about $1/2$ inch from the edge. Sew around only 2 sides.

3. Turn the bag inside out, and pack it loosely with dried beans or peas.

4. Turn the top edges in toward each other, about $1/2$ inch from the edge, and pin them. Sew them together with the whipstitch on page 5.

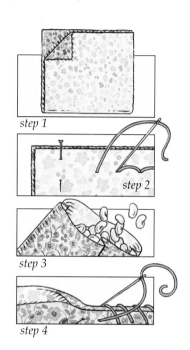

step 1

step 2

step 3

step 4

Beanbag Contest

Divide everyone into 2 teams. Each team forms a line, facing each other. At one end of each line, place a basket. At the other end of each line, place an equal number of bean-bags. At a signal, players pass the beanbags down the line as fast as possible. When the bags reach the end, they are tossed into the basket. If a player drops a beanbag, the bag goes back to the beginning. The team that gets all their beanbags into their basket first wins.

Samantha's Vic

Invite your friends to an elegant

Samantha and her friends loved to have late afternoon tea parties. They gathered to talk, drink tea, and nibble on dainty sweets. Sometimes they even had themed tea parties, like a garden tea party or a doll tea party.

Miss Monica Mayer requests the pleasure of your company on Saturday afternoon, May 26, from two to four o'clock at Samantha's Victorian Tea Party at 2 Monroe Street.

Carolyn

rian Party

ty on the porch!

Victorian Scrap Invitation

For each invitation, use a 7-by-7-inch piece of heavy paper. Glue on a 1-inch border of *scraps*, or colorful pictures. Write your invitation on a 5-by-5-inch piece of white paper. Glue it in the center of the card. Trim the card with lace.

Pressed-Flower Name Cards

Follow the directions on page 60 to press flowers. The day before the party, glue a few pressed flowers on the front of a name card, leaving room for the guest's name. Write your guest's name on the card.

Butterfly Napkin Rings

Attach silk butterflies from a craft store to florist's wire. Wrap the wire around a folded napkin. The butterflies will look like they're fluttering across the table!

55

Teatime Treats

These scrumptious sweets are tasty with tea.

These bite-size cookies are like mini fruit tarts.

Jam Tart Cookies

You will need:

 An adult to help you

Ingredients:
1/4 cup jam
1 cup butter, softened
1/3 cup sugar
1 3/4 cups flour
Pinch of salt

Equipment:
Measuring cups and spoons
Spoon
Small bowl
2 mixing bowls
2 wooden spoons
Baking sheet
Potholders

Directions:

1. Preheat the oven to 350°. Spoon the jam into a small bowl and stir it until it is smooth. Set aside.

2. In a mixing bowl, cream the butter and sugar together until they are light and fluffy.

3. In a separate bowl, mix together the flour and salt. Add the flour mixture to the butter mixture and blend until a dough is formed.

4. Pinch off bits of dough and roll them into 1-inch balls. Place the balls on a baking sheet about 1 inch apart.

5. Press your finger into the center of each cookie to make a "well." If the dough cracks, pinch it back together. Fill each well with 1/4 teaspoon of jam.

6. Bake the cookies for about 10 minutes. Remove from oven and let cool.

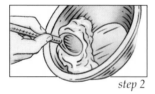
step 2

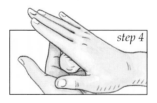
step 4

step 5

Victoria Sponge

This cake was named for Queen Victoria because it was her favorite teatime treat! Make or buy a 2-layer sponge cake. Spread one cake with a layer of jam. Place the other cake on top. Cut the cake into long pieces and arrange them on a plate.

Ice Cream Bombes

Use paper towels to wipe the insides of mini molds with salad oil. Spoon softened ice cream into the molds, and put them into the freezer to harden. Then remove them from the freezer and turn the ice cream onto pretty plates. Decorate with raspberries.

Cucumber Sandwiches

Spread softened cream cheese or butter on a piece of thinly sliced white bread. Place slices of cucumber on the bread. Top it off with another slice of bread, and trim off the crusts. Cut the sandwich into 4 dainty triangles, and add a cucumber slice on top.

Hot Tea Punch

In a saucepan, combine:

- $2^1/_4$ cups sugar
- 2 cups cold water
- 1 lemon rind

Heat the mixture over medium heat and bring it to a boil. Pour 4 cups of boiling water into a mixing bowl. Hang 4 tea bags over the bowl edge, and let the tea steep for about 5 minutes. Take the tea bags out. Add:

- 2 cups orange juice
- $^1/_2$ cup lemon juice
- sugar mixture to taste

Stir well and pour into pretty teacups.

Parlor Pastimes

Play these Victorian games for ladylike fun.

Taboo

Taboo means forbidden. Decide on a letter of the alphabet that will be taboo. One player asks the girl on her left a question. If the girl answers the question without using any word containing the taboo letter, she then asks the player on *her* left a question. Keep going around the circle. When someone uses the forbidden letter, she has to pay a penalty, like singing a silly song.

Throwing the Smile

All the players sit in a circle. One player smiles for 10 seconds. Then she wipes her hand across her face to "wipe off" the smile and "throws it" to another player. The chosen player has to catch the smile in her hand, put it on, wear it, and wipe it off to throw to someone else. If a player smiles out of turn, she is out. The players who are out must try hard to make the other players smile!

Whispers

All the players sit in a circle. One person starts by whispering a short story to the girl next to her. Whisper the story around the circle until it reaches the last girl. Then the last girl tells her story to the group. It's fun to see how different that story is from the original!

HAVE A SING

In the early 1900s, the parlor was the most important room of the house. Some people entertained guests in their parlor by gathering around the piano and "having a sing." Popular songs in 1904 included "A Bicycle Built for Two" and "Sweet Adeline." You can find turn-of-the-century music for your party at your local library.

These girls are having a doll tea party in 1902.

Read Tea Leaves

Brew a pot of tea with loose tea leaves. Pour the tea into teacups. While you drink the tea, think of a question. Just for fun, when your cup is almost empty, swirl the tea around. Then turn it upside down on its saucer. Pick up the cup and look at the leaves that are still inside.

If most of the leaves are near the rim of the cup, the answer to your question is "soon."

If most of the leaves are in the center, the answer is "far in the future."

If most of the leaves are near the handle of the cup, the answer is "yes."

If most of the leaves are far from the handle, the answer is "no."

Use your imagination to read the tea leaves. If the leaves are shaped like animals, letters, or numbers, work that into your answer!

Tea Table

All the players form a circle. Each player takes the name of an item found on a tea table, such as Tea, Toast, Butter, Sugar, or Cream. The player named Tea starts. She stands in the center of the circle, turns around on one foot, and says, "I turn Tea, who turns Sugar?" Tea moves back out to the circle, and Sugar turns on one foot and answers, "I turn Sugar, who turns Cream?" The game keeps going until a player forgets her name or does not answer right away. She then has to pay a penalty, like patting her head and rubbing her stomach at the same time while standing on one leg.

Teapot

One player leaves the room, while the other players decide on words that sound the same, but have more than one meaning. Some words are: *two/to/too*, *for/four*, *so/sew*, and *pear/pair*. When the player is called in, her job is to figure out the chosen word. The other players talk about the word, but use the word *teapot* in its place. For example, if the words chosen are *two/to/too*, the players might say:

"I have *teapot* (two) hands."

"I am going *teapot* (to) school today."

"I have *teapot* (two) hands, *teapot* (too)."

When the player guesses the hidden words, a new player leaves the room and the game begins again.

Victorian Crafts

Samantha and her friends delighted in making pretty projects like these at their parties.

Victorians liked to bring nature into their homes by decorating with flowers and leaves.

step 2

steps 3 and 4

Fern Candle

You will need:

An adult to help you
Newspapers
1-pound box paraffin wax
Empty tin can
Saucepan

Water
Pillar candles
Pressed fern leaves
(see below)
Paintbrush

Directions:

1. Spread newspapers over your work space.

2. Have an adult put the paraffin in the can and the can in the saucepan. Fill the saucepan halfway with water. Boil the water in the pan. *Watch the paraffin carefully.* Once it has melted, take the saucepan off the stove.

3. Hold a candle on its side and place a pressed leaf on it. Dip the paintbrush in the melted paraffin.

4. Carefully brush a thin layer of paraffin over the leaf to glue it to the side of the candle. If your paintbrush hardens, dip it in the warm paraffin.

5. Continue placing leaves and painting them down. The paraffin will cool quickly, so you may need to melt it more than once.

Pressed Flowers and Fern Leaves

A week before your party, gather flowers and leaves to press. Arrange them between 2 sheets of newspaper. Lay a stack of heavy books over them and let them dry for several days. Be sure the flowers and leaves are flat and dry before you use them. They're great for decorating cards, notebooks, bookmarks, and more.

Sketchbook

You will need:

2 pieces of heavy paper, 6 by 9 inches
Ruler
Pencil
Scissors
Masking tape
3 pieces of 8½-by-11-inch paper, cut in half
Hole punch
Ribbon
Pressed flowers, colored pencils, crayons *(optional)*

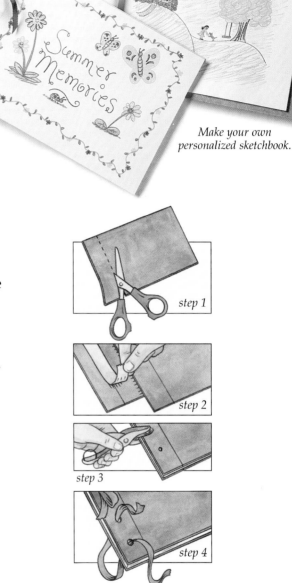

Make your own personalized sketchbook.

Directions:

1. The pieces of heavy paper are the covers of the book. To make a binding, measure a 1-inch-wide strip on the short side of each cover. Cut off the strips.

   step 1

2. Tape each strip back in place with masking tape. Turn the covers over so the masking tape is on the inside.

   step 2

3. Stack the other paper between the covers. Use the hole punch to punch 4 holes along the strip.

   step 3

4. Thread ribbon through the holes and tie bows. Decorate your cover with pressed flowers, a drawing, or anything else you wish.

   step 4

VICTORIAN FLOWERS

*In Victorian times, girls and women rambled the countryside with manuals to identify the flowers they found. When they got home they often wanted to **preserve**, or keep, the flowers. They pressed the flowers and mounted them in frames and scrapbooks. They also dried whole bouquets and kept them under glass domes.*

Samantha's Nutting Party

Gather your friends and go nuts!

Squirrel Invitation

For each invitation, fold a 9-by-12-inch piece of brown construction paper in half to make a card. Trace the squirrel pattern from page 89, and cut it out. Line up the squirrel's tail along the folded edge of the card. Tape the pattern in place, and cut out the squirrel. Add a construction paper nut if you like! Write the invitation inside.

Nutty Party Favors

Before the party, crack open one walnut for each guest. Save the nuts for Nut-Crunch Apples (page 63). Line the shells with foil, and put small charms inside. Glue the walnuts back together, and let dry. Then glue on ribbon and lace. When they're dry, put them in a pretty dish on your party table. After your meal, have each guest crack open a nut to find a surprise.

Walnut Shell Fortunes

Before the party, write a fortune for each guest on a small piece of paper. Roll up the fortune, and tie it in the middle with a long piece of string. Place the ends of the string in a bowl of water so the fortunes dangle around the outside of the bowl. Then make a walnut boat for each person. Put putty or clay in half of a walnut shell, and stick a toothpick in it. On a paper sail, write your guest's name. Glue the sail onto the toothpick. When your guests arrive, let each girl sail her boat to see which fortune it chooses.

Nut-Crunch Apples

Cut 4 medium cooking apples in half with a knife. Remove the apple cores with a melon baller or a spoon. In a small bowl, mix together 4 tablespoons each of currants and walnuts. Then add 2 tablespoons each of brown sugar and butter. Spoon the mixture into the apple halves. Place the apple halves in a skillet, stuffed side up. Add 2 cups of apple juice to the skillet. Cover and simmer the apples for 15 minutes, or until they are tender.

Nut Sandwiches

In a small mixing bowl, mix 4 tablespoons of finely chopped walnuts and 1/4 pound of softened cream cheese. Spread the mixture on a slice of bread. Top it off with another slice of bread, and trim off the crusts. Cut the sandwich into 4 dainty triangles.

Apple Cider

In a medium saucepan, heat 1 quart apple cider, 1/2 teaspoon allspice, 3 whole cloves, and 1 cinnamon stick. Heat the mixture over medium heat for 5 minutes. Add 1/4 cup brown sugar, and bring the mixture to a boil. Heat it for 5 more minutes. Serve the cider hot with a cinnamon stick stirrer.

NUTTING PARTIES

Fall nutting parties were popular at the turn of the century. Girls wandered into the woods with baskets slung over their arms, ready to collect the nuts that had fallen from the trees. Or, they'd shake the trees to get the nuts to fall! They gathered hickory nuts, walnuts, beechnuts, butternuts, and hazelnuts. The one nut they didn't find was the peanut. It grows underground!

Samantha's Painting Party

Invite your friends over for an artistic afternoon.

Framed Invitation

For each invitation, you will need a 5-by-7-inch unlined index card. Cut up gold doilies, and glue them around the edges of the card to make a frame. Write your invitation on the card.

Painted Cookies

Make your favorite sugar cookie dough, or use a tube of refrigerated cookie dough. Bake the cookies according to the directions. Use decorator icing or gel to paint the cookies. Use painting styles popular during Samantha's time, like *impressionism* (broad strokes and dabs of bright paint) or *pointillism* (dots of color side by side).

Artist's Palette Cake

Bake your favorite cake in a 9-by-13-inch pan. Let the cake cool, then freeze it the night before the party. In the morning, take the cake out of the freezer. Have an adult cut the cake so it looks like an artist's *palette*, or tray for mixing colors. Frost the cake with white frosting. Use different colors of frosting for paint dabs, and add brushes for a final artistic touch.

Water Color

Pour sparkling white grape juice for each guest. Let guests add their own food coloring. If you like, use new paintbrushes for swizzle sticks.

These young ladies from 1909 are acting out "Farewell to the Mayflower."

Drawing Game

One player draws the head of a person, an animal, or a bird, and folds the paper over, leaving only a mark where the neck is. The next player draws a body and folds it over. The third person draws the legs. See what kind of creature you come up with!

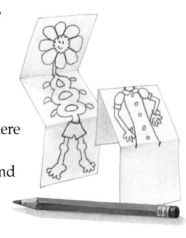

Tableaux Vivants (tab-LOH vee-VAHN)

Tableaux vivants means "living pictures" in French. All the players divide into 2 teams. Team A poses as a famous painting or sculpture, or as a scene from a well-known book. Team A lets Team B know if they are posing from a painting, sculpture, or book. Team B tries to guess what they are. When Team B guesses correctly, it's their turn to pose.

Paint on Glass

Use Liquitex Glossies paints (available at craft stores) to paint designs on a glass bottle. Let the paint dry, then bake your masterpiece according to the instructions on the paint jars.

VICTORIAN PAINTING

A young lady's paint box might have a brush, tubes of paint, a palette, and a color chart that taught how to mix and match colors. It was important to **set the palette,** *or keep the colors in the same place on the palette, so she wouldn't have to look down at them while she was busy painting a scene.*

This paint box is from the turn of the century.

Molly's Home

Parties on the home front were r

Parties during World War Two were simpler than parties before the war. Many foods were rationed, and people were busy with wartime jobs. Still, parties helped raise spirits. As the war came to an end, Americans had more reasons than ever to celebrate. Whole towns greeted their heroes and heroines with victory parades and entertained them with talent shows.

Come to Molly's Home-front Party
dll's house,
n Lane,
April 28
oo.

Front Party

ite, and true blue!

GETTING STARTED

V-Mail Invitation

During the war, people used *V-mail*, or Victory mail, to write to soldiers. Fold a 6-by-10-inch piece of red construction paper into thirds. Open it up, write the invitation on the inside, and then close it. Trace the V pattern from page 90, and cut it out. Tape it to a piece of blue construction paper. Cut out the V, and then glue it to the outside of the card.

Star Name Cards

For each name card, trace the star pattern from page 92. Tape it to colored paper. Cut it out. Write a name on it and decorate with markers and glitter.

Hanging Flags

Trace the star and flag patterns from page 90. Tape them to red, white, or blue paper. Cut them out. 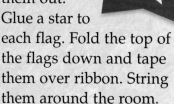 Glue a star to each flag. Fold the top of the flags down and tape them over ribbon. String them around the room.

Food for Victory

Even war rationing didn't stop Molly from making sweet treats!

Families like Molly's learned how to make do without rationed foods like sugar. This pie recipe was a favorite for wartime cooks.

Sugarless Apple Pie

You will need:

An adult to help you

Ingredients:

1 cup light corn syrup
4 tablespoons flour
5 or 6 apples
Folded pre-made piecrusts
2 tablespoons butter
1/2 teaspoon cinnamon

Equipment:

Saucepan
Measuring cups and spoons
Wooden spoon
Apple peeler and corer
Knife
Pie pan
Potholders

Directions:

1. In a saucepan, combine the corn syrup and flour. Heat over medium heat and stir until the mixture is smooth and thick. Let cool.

2. Peel and core the apples. Then slice the apples into rings. Follow the directions on the piecrust box to place 1 sheet of pastry in a pie pan.

3. Layer the apples in the pie. Pour the syrup mixture over the apples. Dot the apples with butter, and sprinkle on cinnamon.

4. To place the top crust, follow the directions on the piecrust box for the 2-crust pie. Bake the pie at 425° for 30 to 40 minutes. Remove from oven and let cool before serving.

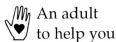
step 2

step 3

step 4

Quick Chocolate Cake

You will need:

 An adult
to help you

Ingredients:

2²/₃ cups flour
4 teaspoons baking powder
1 teaspoon baking soda
1 cup plus 5 tablespoons sugar
4 tablespoons water
10 tablespoons semisweet cocoa
¹/₂ cup butter, softened
2 eggs
1 cup milk
2 teaspoons vanilla
Chocolate frosting

Equipment:

2 mixing bowls
Measuring cups
  and spoons
Small saucepan
2 wooden spoons
2 layer-cake pans,
  greased
Potholders
Knife or small
  spatula

Families often saved their supply of sugar so they could make a treat like this for a special occasion. This recipe was quick and easy for busy war workers.

Directions:

1. In a mixing bowl, combine the flour, baking powder, and baking soda. Set aside.

2. In a saucepan, combine 4 tablespoons of sugar, the water, and the cocoa. Melt the mixture on medium heat for 1 minute, stirring constantly.

step 2

3. In a separate mixing bowl, cream the butter and the rest of the sugar together. Add the eggs. Beat well. Add the flour mixture to the creamed mixture.

4. Add the cocoa mixture, the milk, and the vanilla. Pour the batter into the pans. Bake at 350° for 20 minutes. Remove from oven and let cool. Frost with chocolate frosting.

step 4

Fruit Fizz

Fill a glass halfway with your favorite fruit juice. Then add ginger ale until it almost reaches the top. Add a scoop of vanilla ice cream if you wish.

Fun and Games

Some of Molly's favorite games are still popular today.

Musical Flags

Before the party, hide tiny flags around the room. When it's time to play, all the players sit in a circle. Then play patriotic music, like "The Star-Spangled Banner." When the music stops, the players gather as many flags as they can before the music starts again. When it starts, the player with the most flags wins!

Flag Relay

Divide the players into teams, with 3 or 4 runners per team. Line the runners from each team along a race route, with about 25 yards between each racer. The first runner for each team has a flag to pass. At the starting signal, she sprints to the second player in line. When she reaches her, she passes the flag, and the second runner dashes for the third, who then passes it to the fourth. The fourth runner heads for the finish line. If a runner drops the flag, her team is out. The first team to reach the finish without dropping the flag wins.

Prisoner's Base

Use chalk to mark off a court about 30 by 50 feet. Draw a line down the middle and mark off opposite corners as "prisons." The players form 2 teams, and each chooses a side of the court. At a signal, each team moves into the other's territory. The object of the game is to capture all the members of the opposite team by tagging them. Once players are in enemy territory, they can be tagged and put in prison. They can be freed by another team member who gets into the prison without being tagged. The team that captures all of the players on the opposite team first wins.

Statues

One player is the Sculptor. The Sculptor twirls each player around twice, then lets go. The player freezes into a statue form. The Statues hold their positions until all the players have been twirled. Then the Sculptor chooses a favorite Statue to become the next Sculptor.

Red Rover

One player is Red Rover. She stands in the middle of the yard. The other players form a line on one side of her. Red Rover chooses a player and calls, "Red Rover, Red Rover, let *Molly* cross over!" That player runs to the opposite side of the yard. If Red Rover catches her, she must help Red Rover catch another player. The game is over when everyone is caught.

Pom-Pom-Pull-Away

Make a goal line at each end of the playground. Split up into 2 groups. Each group stands behind a goal line. One person stands alone in the middle as "It." It calls, "Pom-Pom-Pull-Away, come away or I'll fetch you away." All the players run across to the opposite goal while It tries to tag them. The players who are tagged stand in the middle with It. Repeat the game until all of the players are in the middle. To start the next game, the first person who was tagged is the new It.

ROLLER-SKATING

During the war, factories stopped making toys like roller skates and started making war equipment. Skates like Molly's had a skate key that loosened or tightened the skates to fit different shoe sizes. One pair of skates could last through lots of growing!

Home-Front Handicrafts

Molly and her friends made toys from scraps around the house.

Kaleidoscope

To work the kaleidoscope, face a window and look into the open end of the tube. Slowly turn the kaleidoscope. What do you see?

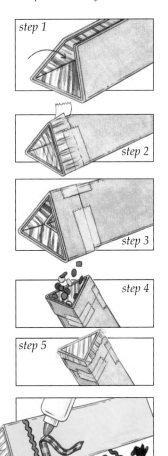

step 1

step 2

step 3

step 4

step 5

step 6

You will need:

Scissors	Tape
Ruler	Clear plastic bag
Pencil	Transparent beads,
Mylar*	shiny confetti
Tagboard	Tracing paper
Rubber cement	Colored paper

*Available at paper- and party-supply stores.

Directions:

1. Cut a 4½-by-8-inch piece of Mylar and of tagboard. Glue them together using rubber cement. Fold the piece into 3 equal parts with the Mylar on the inside. Tape the edges together.

2. Cut a piece of plastic from the bag so it fits over one end of the tube. Tape it down.

3. Cut a 5-by-1-inch piece of Mylar and of tagboard. Glue them together. Tape the strip around the tube so it sticks out over the covered end. The Mylar should be on the inside.

4. Hold the tube upright with the short piece of tube at the top. Drop in the beads and confetti.

5. Cut out a triangular piece of tracing paper. Tape it down over the filled end of the tube.

6. Cut a piece of colored paper 5 by 8 inches. Glue it around the tube. Decorate the tube if you wish.

Marbles

You will need:

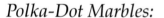 An adult
to help you
Polymer clay in different colors
(Fimo or Sculpey)*
Glass baking dish

Available at craft stores.

Swirl Marbles:

1. Roll 2 ropes ¼ inch wide from different clay colors. Twist the ropes together. Use your fingers to blend the twist together until the colors start to streak.

2. Pinch off 5 inches of rope for a large marble, 3 inches for a small one. Roll into balls.

step 1

step 2

Polka-Dot Marbles:

1. Make one 1-inch-wide ball and several tiny balls of other colors. Lightly press the colored balls onto the large ball. Roll the ball gently to smooth it.

step 1

Spiral Marbles:

1. Make one 1-inch-wide ball. Roll 2 thin ropes from different colors. Twist the 2 ropes together. Wrap the rope around the ball. Roll the ball gently to smooth it.

step 1

Note:

After all the marbles are made, place them in the glass baking dish. Bake them for 10 minutes at 275°. Let the marbles cool completely before removing them from the dish.

Shoot Marbles

Hold the marble between your first finger and your middle finger. Lightly press the knuckles of your first finger to the ground. Use your thumb to flick the marble out of your hand and toward the target.

Molly's Summer Camp-Out

Molly loved summer camp. Pitch a tent and invite your friends for your own camp-out!

Come to
Molly's Camp-Out
at Leah's house,
24 Fifth Street,
on Saturday, July 10,
at 4:00.

Tent Invitation

For each invitation, trace the tent pattern from page 91 2 times. Tape the patterns to 2 different colors of construction paper, and cut them out. In one tent, punch holes where the pattern has circles, and then cut on the solid line up the center. Take the other tent and punch only the outer 2 holes, and then squeeze glue around the tent's sides and roof only. Lay the first tent over it so the outer holes line up. Fold up the tent flaps, and tie with string. Write your invitation inside.

Doughboys

Wrap biscuit dough around clean sticks. Pinch the dough together over the ends of the sticks. Place the sticks on a baking sheet. Bake at 375° for 10 minutes or until golden brown. After the sticks have cooled, remove them from the biscuits and fill the holes with butter, jam, peanut butter, or anything else that sounds yummy!

S'mores

Put pieces of chocolate bars on graham crackers. Top with marshmallows. Put them on a plate and microwave on high for 15 to 20 seconds, or until the marshmallows puff up. Add a top cracker to each and press down. Let cool before eating.

Pigs in a Blanket

In a mixing bowl, combine ½ cup shredded cheddar cheese, 1 tablespoon minced onion, 2 tablespoons ketchup, and ½ teaspoon dry mustard. Unroll pre-made crescent dough and separate into triangles. Cut the triangles in half. Spread each triangle with a thin layer of the cheese mixture. Roll them around mini hot dogs. Place them on a baking sheet. Bake at 375° for 10 minutes or until golden. Serve immediately.

Sprint Tug-of-War

Divide into 2 teams. Put a rope on the ground in the middle of a playing field. Each team lines up at opposite ends of the field equally distant from the rope. On *Go,* the teams sprint to the rope and grab it. The first team to get one end of the rope back to its home base wins.

Flashlight Tag

Grab your flashlight for after-dark fun! Choose one person to be "It," and give her the flashlight. She tries to tag another player by shining a flashlight on her and calling out her name. The tagged person becomes the new It.

Pitch a Tent

Between Chairs

Ask your parents for 4 chairs. Drape blankets over the chairs to create your own secret space.

Under a Table

Drape a blanket over a picnic table or a card table. Then crawl inside for some "under-cover" fun!

Between Trees

Tie a rope between 2 trees. Drape a blanket over the rope. Pull the sides of the blanket out and anchor them with rocks.

STARGAZING

In the 1940s, campers studied the stars and learned stories about the constellations. The Big Dipper is part of the constellation **Ursa Major.** *Native Americans called it the Great Bear because it looked like a large bear looking for a place to hibernate. Look for a star guide in your local library and do some gazing yourself!*

Big Dipper

Cassiopeia, the queen

Cygnus, the swan

Molly's Hawaiian Hula Party

Your friends will love this party in paradise!

Palm Tree Invitation

For each invitation, fold a blue piece of construction paper in half. Trace the palm tree pattern from page 92. Tape it to a piece of green construction paper, and cut it out. Add a sandpaper beach and shiny starfish. Write the invitation on the inside.

Come to Molly's
Hawaiian Hula
at Dana's house,
627 Pickford Street,
on Saturday, May 3
at 3:00.

Hawaiian Banana Bread

Mix up your favorite banana bread. Bake it according to the directions. To make the frosting, mix 2 tablespoons milk, 1 teaspoon vanilla, and 1 tablespoon melted butter in a small bowl. Slowly mix in $2\frac{1}{2}$ cups powdered sugar. Mix the frosting until it is thick enough to spread. If it needs more liquid add a little more milk. Drizzle the frosting over the bread. Decorate it with slices of banana, kiwi, or star fruit.

Tropical Twists

For each drink you will need 1 banana, 1 6-ounce can of pineapple juice, 3 teaspoons canned pure coconut milk, and 1 tablespoon sugar. Peel and slice the banana. Place in a blender. Add the pineapple juice, coconut milk, and sugar. Ask an adult to cover the blender and blend until smooth. Refrigerate until it's time to serve.

Fruit Kabobs

Have an adult help you cut fruit like pineapple, watermelon, kiwis, oranges, and bananas into small pieces. Slide them onto wooden skewers in pretty combinations.

Limbo

Have 2 players each hold one end of a yardstick. Each player must pass under it bending backward without touching the floor with her hands or knees. If any part of her body touches the stick, she's out. Lower the stick after everyone has had a turn. See how low you can go!

The Hula

Step right with your right foot. Bring your left foot beside your right. Then step left. Bring your right foot beside your left. Step right and start again. Once you have the steps down, tell a story with your hands. Make up moves, but keep them smooth, simple, and graceful.

Hawaiian Music

HAWAII

In the 1940s, Hawaii became popular as people heard about it on the radio and saw it in motion pictures. It was called the Paradise of the Pacific. After the war, when families were together again and traveling was easier, Hawaii became one of America's top vacation destinations.

Once you and your guests have your hulas down, set them to music. Look for recordings of Hawaiian music at the library.

Lei (lay)

Buy plastic leis at party-supply stores, or scrunch balls of colored tissue paper and string them with a needle and thread.

Hula Skirt

For an easy grass skirt, tuck strips of crepe paper into the waist of a pair of shorts, and swish as you sway!

Patterns

A B C D E F G
H I J K L M
N O P Q R S T
U V W X Y Z

a b c d e f g h i j k l m
n o p q r s t u v w x y z
1 2 3 4 5 6 7 8 9 0

FELICITY'S ALPHABET

78

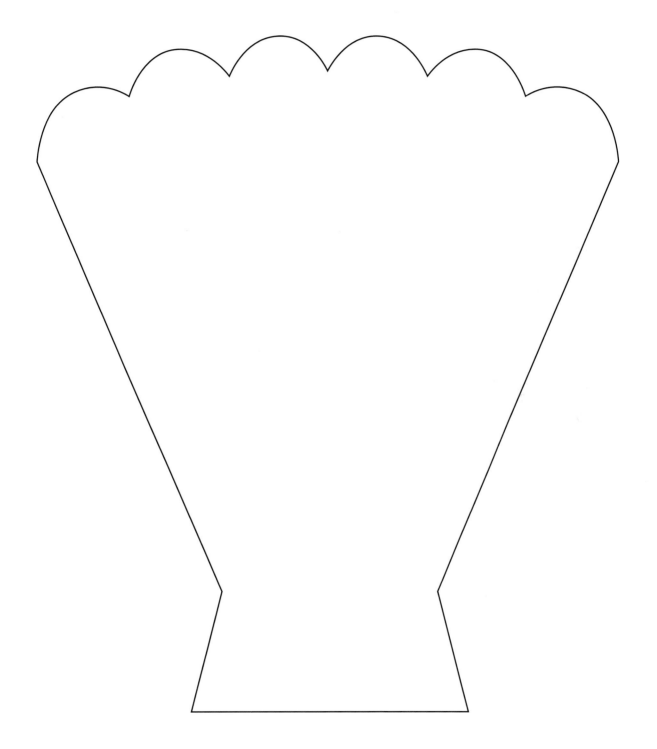

FELICITY'S NEW YEAR'S BALL FAN

lay this edge along the fold

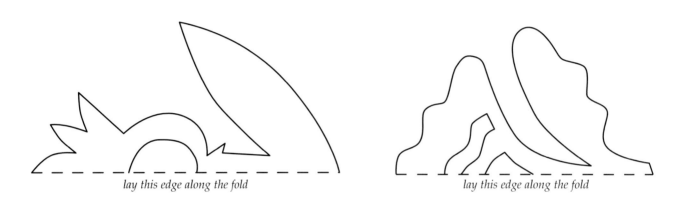

lay this edge along the fold

lay this edge along the fold

FELICITY'S PAPYROTAMIA

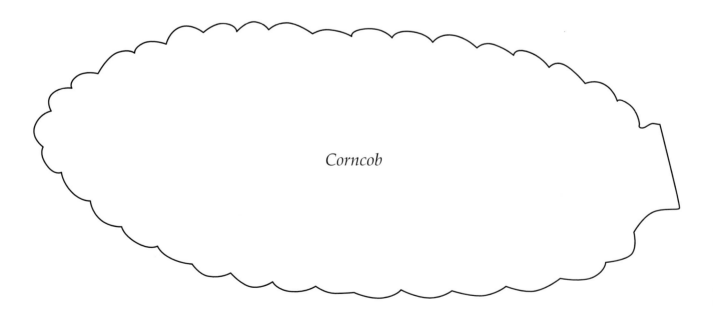

Corncob

JOSEFINA'S CORNHUSK INVITATION

80

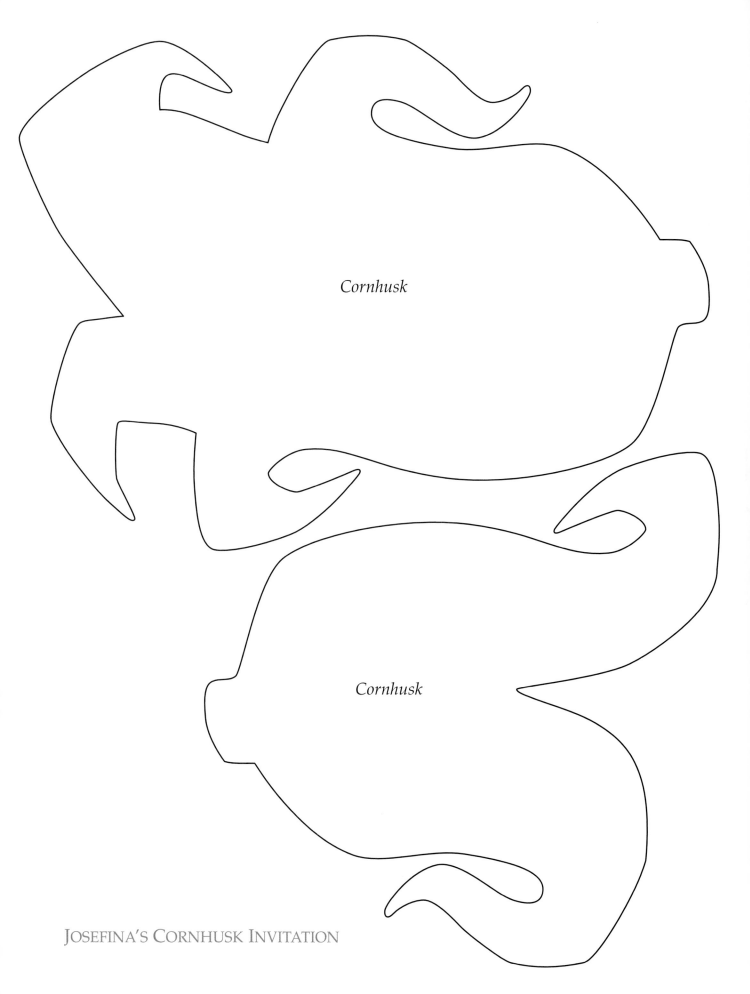

Cornhusk

Cornhusk

JOSEFINA'S CORNHUSK INVITATION

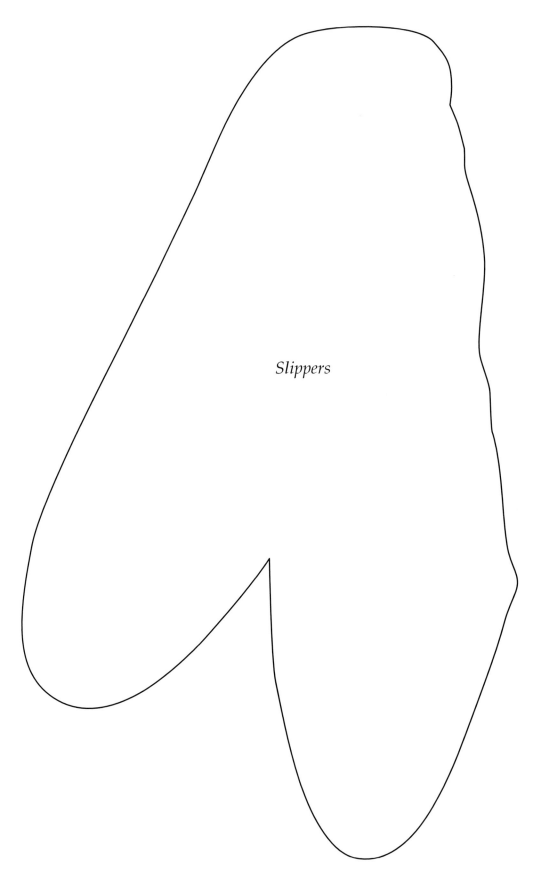

Slippers

JOSEFINA'S FANDANGO INVITATION

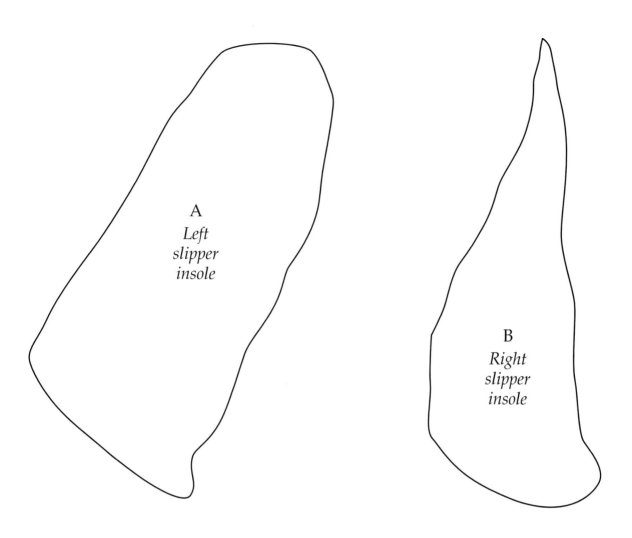

A
*Left
slipper
insole*

B
*Right
slipper
insole*

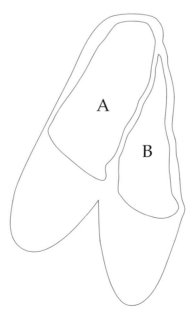

A

B

assemble pieces as shown

lay this edge along the fold

For each invitation, fold a piece of construction paper in half. Trace this pattern onto tracing paper. Place the dotted line along the folded edge of the card. Tape it in place, and cut it out.

JOSEFINA'S RAMILLETE INVITATION

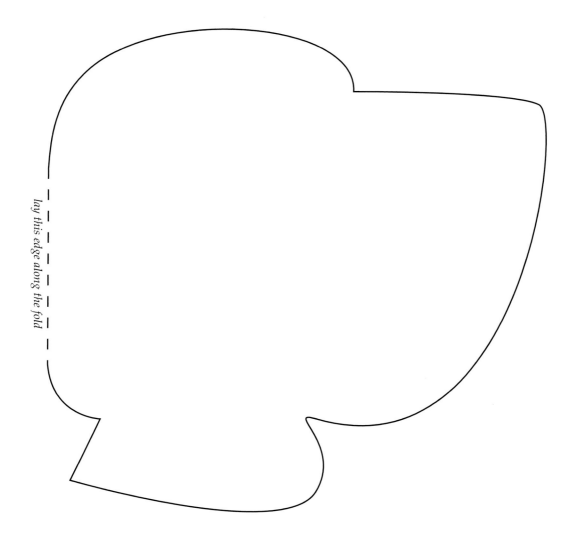

lay this edge along the fold

KIRSTEN'S BONNET INVITATION

Sew around the kitten on this dotted line

leave a gap for stuffing

KIRSTEN'S CALICO KITTEN

Sew around the bean doll on this dotted line

leave a gap for stuffing

ADDY'S BEAN DOLL

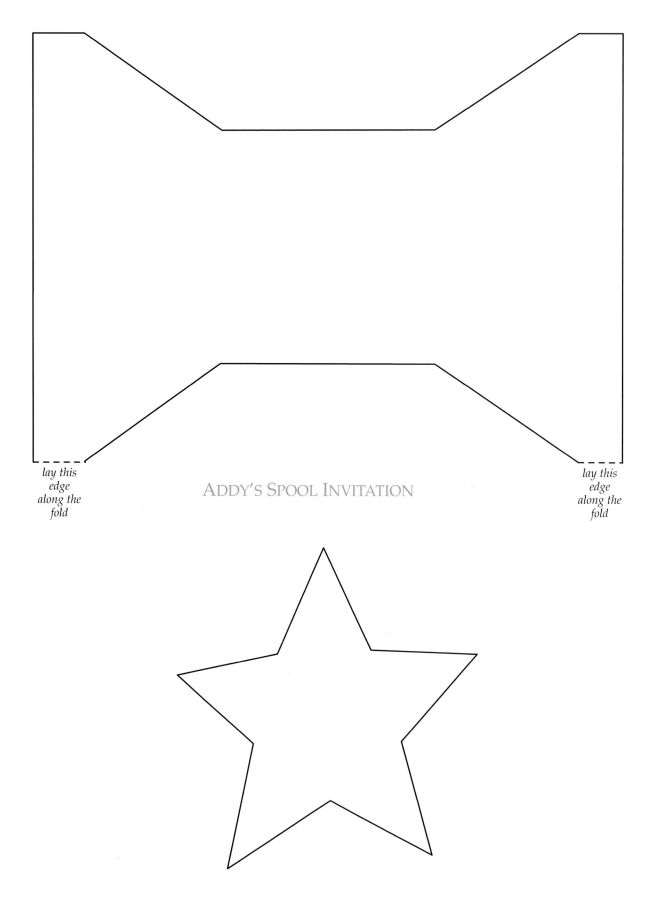